CW00472311

"More than ever, political engagement is vital for businesses as they navigate a complex regulatory environment and seek to manage their reputations. This book captures the need to take that engagement seriously and provides a helpful guide to that important process."

Sir Robbie Gibb, *Former Director of Communications at No. 10 Downing Street and Senior Adviser to Kekst CNC*

"Events around the world confirm almost every day that your organisation's reputation is something you cannot afford to leave unmanaged. No matter what you are doing, or how you try to keep a low profile or avoid controversy, you cannot leave it to manage itself. What you communicate as a leader, and how you communicate it is critical to maintaining a positive reputation with your stakeholders. This book sets out the latest thinking on how to rise to this challenge and shows how investing in good communications will pay you major reputational dividends."

Alastair McCapra, *Chief Executive, Chartered Institute of Public Relations*

"The critical importance of reputation to every organisation has never been clearer: it defines success or failure. This book is the definitive analysis of this vital topic by a world-respected communications expert."

Francis Ingham, *Director General, Public Relations and Communications Association*

REPUTATION IN BUSINESS

A compelling mix of reputation management, crisis leadership and the role of politics in business, this book provides unique practical steps that leaders can take to protect their reputations and those of the organisations they head in an ever more open social media-led world.

Although leaders increasingly recognise the vital intangible asset that reputation represents, too many do not really understand what reputation is and the steps that should be taken to build it and their corporate value. Given the range of factors depending on the organisation, each aspect of its complex reputational story needs to be unpicked if a reputation is to be built, maintained and protected. This step by-step-guide offers advice on how to develop the strategies needed to do this, provides clear lessons throughout from a range of experts – and distinctively, looks beyond the corporate sector to charities, governments, NGOs and the public sector.

Boards, trustees, non-executive directors, senior management and leaders of all types of organisations need to consider the steps that should be taken to build, maintain and defend their reputation, and that means knowing what their reputation is and the audiences that matter most to them. This book is the roadmap.

Stuart Thomson is a public affairs and communications specialist, published author and blogger. He leads the public affairs consultancy at law firm BDB Pitmans, has appeared on Sky News, BBC 5 Live, BBC World and BBC Radio 4's *Today* programme, and has been a judge for the Public Affairs News, PR Week, Public Affairs and the European Public Affairs awards. He was listed as one of the Top 100 Public Affairs Consultants by *Total Politics*, shortlisted for the Institute of Directors and Chartered Institute of Public Relations Director of the Year award, and won the Best Current Affairs Influencer category at Vuelio's Online Influence Awards 2020. Stuart is also an honorary research fellow at the University of Aberdeen.

REPUTATION IN BUSINESS

Lessons for Leaders

Stuart Thomson

Routledge
Taylor & Francis Group

NEW YORK AND LONDON

Cover image: kokouu (Getty Images)

First published 2023
by Routledge
605 Third Avenue, New York, NY 10158

and by Routledge
4 Park Square, Milton Park, Abingdon, Oxon, OX14 4RN

Routledge is an imprint of the Taylor & Francis Group, an informa business

© 2023 Stuart Thomson

The right of Stuart Thomson to be identified as author of this work has
been asserted in accordance with sections 77 and 78 of the Copyright,
Designs and Patents Act 1988.

All rights reserved. No part of this book may be reprinted or reproduced or
utilised in any form or by any electronic, mechanical, or other means, now
known or hereafter invented, including photocopying and recording, or in
any information storage or retrieval system, without permission in writing
from the publishers.

Trademark notice: Product or corporate names may be trademarks or
registered trademarks, and are used only for identification and explanation
without intent to infringe.

Library of Congress Cataloging-in-Publication Data
Names: Thomson, Stuart (Public affairs consultant), author.
Title: Reputation in business : lessons for leaders / Stuart Thomson.
Description: New York, NY : Routledge, 2023.
Identifiers: LCCN 2022012829 | ISBN 9781032277509 (hardback) | ISBN
9781032277462 (paperback) | ISBN 9781003293880 (ebook)
Subjects: LCSH: Corporate image. | Corporations--Public relations. |
Organizational effectiveness.
Classification: LCC HD59.2.T46 2023 | DDC 659.2--dc23/eng/20220317
LC record available at https://lccn.loc.gov/2022012829

ISBN: 9781032277509 (hbk)
ISBN: 9781032277462 (pbk)
ISBN: 9781003293880 (ebk)

DOI: 10.4324/9781003293880

Typeset in Joanna
by Deanta Global Publishing Services, Chennai, India

This book is dedicated to Alex, Will, Callum and Elenya.
But never ignoring Mum, Dad and Iain!

CONTENTS

FOREWORD

The ideas behind this book have been in gestation for some time. The issue of reputation management has become a mainstay of a lot of the work that I do across communications, not least public affairs and political engagement. It always annoyed me slightly that reputation management seemed to be most closely associated with those who deal with the media. I have always believed that it is much broader than that.

Part of the trouble with a media-centric view of reputation management appears to come from some of the writing on the issues involved. This book is my attempt to help broaden the perspective, but to do so in a very practical and hands-on way. If a business leader picks up a copy of this book (Thank you!), they can take some lessons from it which can be applied in their day-to-day role.

The book contains some media, social media and politics all mixed up, which I hope delivers a more rounded approach to reputation management.

I am, as always, enormously grateful for the support of my family (my wife Alex, and children Will, Callum and Elenya). They allowed me the time and space to devote to writing the book. Writing does take time away from family life and proves a distraction, but I hope that they agree that all the hard work has been worth it.

My mum, dad and brother (Bill, Maureen and Iain) also keep me on my toes, asking after the progress of the work, so they provide a clear incentive to finish what I have started.

Much of this book was written during the first COVID-19 lockdown and the extended period of working from home. Somewhat counterintuitively, this seemed to make the task of settling down in the evenings to work on it tougher. But at least I will have something to show for COVID!

I also have to say a massive thank you to all those who have contributed their time and thoughts to this book. They really help bring the book to life and give it voices other than just my own. I hope it is also a reflection of the very nature of reputation management, that no one person can claim to fully understand every aspect. Rather, it is about having a broad understanding and then learning from others. That is certainly what I have tried to do with this book. I also wanted to bring in a range of voices, and I hope I have succeeded in doing that. Thank you for their fantastic contributions to Andrew Hawkins, Gavin Davis, Steve Looney, Lindsey Annable, Ben Lloyd, Tom Jenkin, Pauliina Murphy, Carolina Gasparoli, Catie Shavin, Bene't Steinberg, Gemma Holding, Kirsty McHugh, James White, Isla Reynolds, Chloe Stables, Iain Anderson, Iana Vidal, Daniel Stainsby, Philip Collins, Sarah Atkinson and Adeela Warley OBE.

Thank you also to Matthew Smith at Exprimez. Matthew is ever supportive and encouraging, giving advice when needed. Most importantly, he sold the idea of the book to the fabulous Meredith Norwich at Routledge. What more could you want from a perfect literary agent? Without Matthew, Meredith and the team at Routledge, this script would still be sitting on my hard drive.

As always with my books, faults and failings remain my own, and I would be delighted to receive feedback from everyone who reads this.

Thank you all.

Stuart Thomson
March 2022
www.stuartthomson.co.uk

INTRODUCTION

The issue of reputation is one of the most important facing the leadership team of any organisation. The trouble is that what a reputation is and what should be done about it are much less clear. Equally unclear is who should be responsible for managing an organisation's reputation. This all brings with it an increased level of risk, and unmanaged or undermanaged risk, for any organisation, is fundamentally unhealthy.

There are numerous studies that rank organisations for the strength of their reputation:

The Reputation Institute *Global RepTrak 100*[1]
- Lego, Rolex, Ferrari, Bosch Group, Harley-Davidson, Canon, Adidas, Walt Disney, Microsoft, Sony.

The *Axios Harris Poll 100* (US)[2]
- Patagonia, Honda Motor Company, Moderna, Chick-fil-A, SpaceX, Chewy, Pfizer, Tesla Motors, Costco, Amazon.com.

Fortune[3]
- Apple, Amazon, Microsoft, Walt Disney, Starbacks, Berkshire Hathaway, Alphabet, JPMorgan Chase, Netflix, Costco Wholesale.

DOI: 10.4324/9781003293880-1

YouGov BrandIndex (UK and Ireland)[4]
- Netflix, Marks & Spencer, Cadbury, John Lewis, Visa, IKEA, Royal Mail, Boots, Lindt, Samsung.

Brand Finance *Brand Directory*[5]
- Apple, AmazonVerizon, WeChat., Google, Microsoft, Samsung, Walmart, Facebook, ICBC, Verizon, WeChat.

For the UK, they suggest the top ten most valuable brands are:
- Shell, BP, EY, Vodafone, HSBC, Tesco, Barclays, Sky, Land Rover and Aviva.

All of these studies, and others, have their own methodologies which they claim are better and more accurate. What many of these rankings have in common is that they are conducted and produced as a way of selling reputation enhancing services – "If you want to do better in next year's poll, then contact us for advice …".

That is not to criticise their quality or worth, but instead the emphasis should be on doing your own work on reputation tracking. You can guarantee that any of the companies appearing in the types of studies mentioned all invest time and effort in understanding and managing their reputations. By conducting your own research, you can choose how you are measured. But critically, you can then take decisions about where you need to concentrate future activity.

Reputation should initially be about gathering information, so that you know more about yourself so you are in an informed position to address weaknesses and make the most of strengths.

Reputation benefits

Whilst there may be some discussions about the relative merit of general surveys of reputation, there is no argument about the benefits of a good reputation and the damage inflicted by a poor reputation.

Let's take a moment to briefly consider some studies that illustrate the benefits.

Let's start with a few that deal with the main issue that often comes immediately to mind – sales.

Reputation is a key part of any buying decision. According to *Unlocking the Value of Reputation*, 87% of consumers around the world claim to take the reputation of a company into consideration when thinking about buying a good or service.[6] Better sales should mean greater profitability. Greater profitability should lead to a higher share price.

Then, if you are the likes of Apple, you have the opportunity to charge a premium for your product, at least in part because of the reputation that you have with consumers. So more profits, increased share price and so on.

But this moves into the online realm as well.

- 85% of consumers trust online reviews as much as personal recommendations. Online reviews help formulate trust, although personal recommendations remain the best way to secure trust.
- Only 5% of people look past the first page of Google.
- 65% of consumers trust search engine results.
- 97% of consumers search online for local businesses.
- Positive reviews make 73% of consumers trust a local business more.
- 49% of consumers need at least a four-star rating before they choose to use a business, and read an average of seven reviews before trusting a business.
- 74% of consumers have greater trust in a company if they read positive reviews.[7]

This means we can start to see the need to unpick reputation. From a relatively simple starting position – a good reputation helps sales – as we drill down, we see additional complexity that needs to be addressed if the initial "simple" statement is to hold true. Each aspect of this complex reputational story needs to be unpicked if an overall reputation is to be built, maintained and protected.

> *Lesson – Reputation management is part of risk management*

Fundamentally, if any leader is failing to give adequate consideration to any aspect of the reputation of the organisation they lead, then they are being negligent. The risk management needs to move away from the headlines and dive into the detail.

Boards, trustees, non-executive directors and any senior management team worth their salaries, or allowances, should be asking the questions, but also looking for leadership on these issues.

But that means knowing and understanding what to do about reputation. That is the aim of this book: to provide lessons for business leaders on reputation management in a very practical way. Of course, there will be some theory along the way, but reputation management is all about the practical realities. This book will look at how others have managed and performed – the good, the bad and the downright terrible – so that everyone can learn lessons to help generate their own ideas and know the questions that they should be asking about their own organisations.

Just taking the example of better sales shows the range of questions that need to be asked. But add to this the other potential benefits of a good reputation – the ability to attract and retain:

- The very best talent.
- Stakeholder support.
- Partnerships, such as commercial joint ventures or across corporate social responsibility (CSR).
- Celebrity endorsements.
- Funds from financial institutions, bodies and individuals.
- Suppliers who want to work with you, which improves the contractual arrangements.

With a strong reputation, you can also look at moving into new markets, launching new products and entering new countries – all because of that firm base you have established.

There are also aspects of reputation management that are self-reinforcing. For instance, your ability to secure positive media and social media coverage is enhanced by an existing good reputation. The subsequent coverage itself is more likely to be positive. Furthermore, this attracts positive coverage, and on it goes.

Then add in what is one of the great unsung aspects of reputation management – the political relations element. Politicians are the audience that can do the most significant long-term damage to any organisation.

They can pass new laws and introduce regulations that have the greatest impact on the way any organisation operates.

The political aspect of reputation management features heavily throughout this book.

Lesson – Reputation management is a self-reinforcing virtuous circle, so set yourself on the right path

---

The flip side

That is all extremely positive. But without a growing or good reputation those benefits are simply not there.

For new organisations, the process of reputation building starts from day one of their operations. They are looking to build those benefits as the organisation grows.

Crisis management is another part of reputation management which attracts widespread attention. But even a crisis is influenced by an existing reputation. A strong reputation with the associated good stakeholder links offers better protection. But start with a poor reputation, and the chances of being able to defend yourself are lessened.

Just as there can be a positive media and social media cycle, there can also be a vicious downward spiral triggered by an initial crisis.

A crisis will damage a reputation, but it will not instantly move from 100 to zero. Instead, it is easier to think, as others have described, of reputation being like a bank account. Every time you take steps to improve your reputation, you are making a deposit. But every time you hit a problem or encounter a crisis, you are making a withdrawal. The bigger the crisis, the bigger the withdrawal. But it would have to be something catastrophic for the account to reach zero in one go. Friends and allies speaking up on your behalf can pay into this reputation bank account or help prevent the withdrawals from being too large. When the account starts to get low, then action is needed.

An important factor to consider is the impact on the current leadership. A crisis will:

- Destroy careers.
- Make it difficult to move on to a good role.
- Make it impossible to deal with anything else as it occurs. It takes over utterly and completely.

Reputation should not be seen as having an on-off switch. It is not something you either have or do not have. It is more subtle than that. Few organisations, if any, have no reputation at all, either positive or negative.

Having a poor reputation with some audiences may mean nothing to others. The positive strength of feeling that they have for the organisation may more than offset any negative views held by others. Think about a company that sells low-priced clothing and whose customers love them for it. Their positive feelings could more than offset problems that other audiences may have with the quality of the supply chain or the price paid to landlords for stores.

Being known as hard-nosed business leaders could cause strife with staff but be beneficial in negotiations with suppliers. There is nothing simple about reputation.

Lesson – A crisis can lead to a self-defeating vicious circle unless challenged

---

Reputation applies to all

This book will look at the impact of reputation on a range of types of organisations, including businesses. The reality is that reputation applies to all. No one should consider themselves immune.

Reputation management is not the sole preserve of the corporate sector. Reputations are not just for businesses; they are for every organisation, every individual, every leader.

Every organisation or individual needs to consider the steps that should be taken to build, maintain and defend their reputation.

That means knowing what their reputation is and the audiences that matter most to them.

Lesson – Reputation applies to all

Another common misconception is that reputation management is about being loud and vocal at all times. Effective reputation management means engagement with stakeholders, but that does not always need to be conducted in public.

Quiet reputation management can be just as effective as a more outward-facing approach. Leaders should not be scared off by thinking that reputation management is all about putting themselves in the spotlight.

The value of reputation

The financial worth of a reputation has been widely estimated in terms of finances, but also the hit taken in the event of a crisis, and how long it can take to be re-established. No self-respecting book on reputation can fail to take the opportunity to cite the quote attributed to Warren Buffett, the American investor: "It takes 20 years to build a reputation and five minutes to ruin it. If you think about that, you'll do things differently."

Adopting a financial measure can bring with it the impression of applying only to businesses. But, as noted, this is very far from the case.

For instance, according to the UK Reputation Dividend Report, as of January 2018, reputations were responsible for £1,062 billion of market capitalisation across the FTSE 350, up 8% over the previous year.

The Weber Shandwick report *The State of Corporate Reputation in 2020: Everything Matters Now* claims that "on average, global executives attribute 63 percent of their company's market value to their company's overall reputation. Additionally, there is an important segment of executives that attributes at least 76 percent of their market value to company reputation."[8]

The research suggests that a reputation is "omnidriven", being influenced by a number of factors with no one factor dominating. As a result, there needs to be a focus on these many drivers of reputation.

The report finds that only 3% of executives believe that their company's reputation is somewhat or very weak, whilst 87% say it is strong, with 45% going further and saying it is very strong.

When asked about the reputations of their CEOs, 82% of global executives think their reputation is strong, with 38% believing it is very strong.

AMO's *What Price Reputation?* includes the findings that corporate reputations account for 35.3% of the market capitalisation of the world's 15 leading equity market indices. This delivers $16.77 trillion of value for shareholders. The report suggested that reputations helped to support corporate value in 2018 as markets came under pressure. Reputation value grew by 2.1% in the 12 months to Q1 2019, whilst the total market capitalisation fell by 0.4%. The report also found that 21% of companies have reputations that are so poor that they actually destroy market capitalisation.

According to *The Economics of Reputation*, a Public Relations and Communications Association survey from 2014, 76% believed that boards perceive a strong link between reputation and financial performance. CEOs see the value of reputation management on the bottom line, but convincing others, such as CFOs, about the worth of reputation can still be a struggle.

This would seem to be borne out by a study of FTSE 350 companies that found that only a third of large corporates in the UK use reputation as a key business driver, with only half of them measuring it and linking it to business outcomes.[9] There remains a lot of work to be done.

The International Communications Consultancy Organisation *World PR Report* for 2020 found that corporate CEOs take reputation seriously, and it was an expected area of growth over the next five years as well as being the biggest area of growth for the previous year.

For those in agencies, the report found that 41% thought that the most important objective for clients' public relations goals was corporate reputation.

When it came to how much reputation and communications challenges are meaningfully considered when setting and reviewing a long-term business strategy, the report found that 33% said "almost always" and 42% "often". But looking by sector, the report suggested some large variation: for instance, from 51% in food/drink/hospitality down to 20% in healthcare, 18% in financial services (and insurance) and 17% in automotive.[10]

In the same report, more than half (59%) of people who trust a company a great deal would be prepared to give them the benefit of the doubt in times of a crisis.[11]

The figure that 90% of an organisation's value is down to intangible assets such as reputation is widely cited. The *Ocean Tomo Intangible Asset Market Value Study* takes as its basis the S&P 500 Market Value.[12] The figure for 2020 is actually up from 2015's 84%, but arguably more important is the significant and continuous upward trend of the value figure for intangible assets.

There has been a shift from tangible to intangible assets for organisations. Back in 2004, a report by the World Economic Forum and Fleishman-Hillard suggested that:

> Three-fifths (59%) of the survey respondents estimated that corporate brand or reputation represents more than 40% of a company's market capitalization. And more than 77% believe that reputation has become more important over the last two years.[13]

The upward trajectory of the figures is undeniable.

The Brand Finance *Global Intangible Finance Tracker*, published in November 2019, tracks intangible elements such as brand, reputation and relationships. As Stuart Bruce suggested when considering an earlier version of the report:

> There is scope for the public relations profession globally to do more on increasing understanding of how PR adds real financial value to the overall business or organisation, not by delivering tactical campaigns, but by enhancing and protecting overall corporate reputation including the reputation of individual brands.[14]

This starts to give you a flavour of the importance of reputation and illustrates why having to deal effectively with any crisis can be so critical.

In a book review, the *Financial Times* expressed the issue starkly: "Unexpected crises can destroy businesses and reputations. Boards, chief executives and their managers may believe they have a firm grip on the risks they face. They should think again."[15]

The book being reviewed, *Rethinking Reputational Risk* by Fitzsimmons and Atkins, suggests that while crises seem to come about swiftly, "most take more than three years to emerge". This points to the heart of reputation management. It is down to decision-making.

A useful weekend exercise is picking an organisation and asking yourself what you think about them and their reputation. Consider everything from what your "gut reaction" is through to what you think the main contributors are to their reputation. Are they up on the up or falling back? Can you put that down to particular incidents or efforts that you think they have made? Maybe you have become more aware of the organisation because of their profile-raising or advertising? Maybe you have seen more of their CEO in recent months?

None of this happens by accident. This is part of their decision-making process.

Lesson – Reputations are the result of deliberate actions or inaction

---

The ongoing challenge

So what should leaders be thinking about?

Reputation management is a topic about which many views can be expressed, and let's not shy away from the fact that you can spend all your time receiving advice on it.

We can all agree that an organisation wants to have a good, positive reputation, but with whom, and what steps do you need to take?

Where this book differs from others is that it takes a very practical approach. The book will not just consider what others do, but will provide ideas that you can take away and use day in, day out.

Whatever type of leader you are, whatever type of organisation you lead, the concept is that this book will be of practical use to you.

The backdrop to all discussions about reputation is that we live in an era of falling trust in government, institutions, the media, businesses, charities and capitalism. Just take a look at the Edelman Trust Barometer, which has been running for over 20 years, and you will see a picture of generally declining trust. The 2020 results highlighted the growth in the sense of inequality as one of the factors driving down trust. The 2021 results showed that the impact of COVID-19 had hit trust still further. For 2022, trust in business had increased in some countries but declined in others, such as the US and UK. However, according the figures, business is more trusted, on the whole, than government.

The Institute of Business Ethics report *Attitudes of the British Public to Business Ethics 2020* shows a more positive picture as far as the British public's attitude towards business behaviour is concerned. The survey does, however, suggest that the public want tax avoidance and environmental responsibility addressed.

According to *Unlocking The Value of Reputation: The Definitive Link Between Corporate Reputation and Better Business Efficiency*, a Game Changers Ipsos report, highly regulated industries are viewed more sceptically than others. That, however, hardly seems surprising. Regulation does not appear from nowhere. There will have been a motivation for regulation in the first place. It is very often the outcome of a perceived market failure, a market abuse or the potential for one. Consumers, the environment and employees are all potential victims, so regulation is seen as the response from governments desperate to show they are taking action.

For as long as capitalism is perceived to be in crisis, the emphasis will be on businesses to reform and make a greater contribution.

Often an issue will start as being only, or mainly, relevant to one sector. The environment was initially of primary interest to oil and gas companies and the extraction industry. It was a failing associated with them. Now all organisations are expected to play a role in tackling climate change. It applies to us all.

Leaders should never assume that an issue will forever be the preserve of just one sector. Expectations change amongst a range of stakeholders, and it is up to leaders to know, understand and take action. Ideally, action should be taken pre-emptively as this offers opportunities to strengthen a reputation. Being ahead of the game is always preferable to being forced into action.

Expectations evolve and higher standards become a benchmark by which others are judged. As companies set exacting standards for environmental protection and workplace relations, then the same starts to be expected of the public sector and charities. Campaigning groups and individuals apply pressure, as can the media and government.

> *Lesson – Reputation management looks inside as well as out*

As we will see throughout this book, a leader needs to push and challenge when it comes to reputation. Standing still can be dangerous.

Notes

1 The Reputation Institute (2021) (www.reputationinstitute.com/global-reptrak-100).
2 The Harris Poll (2021) (https://theharrispoll.com/axios-harrispoll-100/).
3 Fortune (2021) (https://fortune.com/worlds-most-admired-companies/).
4 YouGov (2021) (www.brandindex.com).
5 Brand Finance (2021) (https://brandirectory.com).
6 Game Changers Ipsos (2018).
7 Campbell (2020) (https://blog.reputationx.com/online-reputation-management-statistics).
8 Weber Shandwick (2020) (www.webershandwick.com/wp-content/uploads/2020/01/The-State-of-Corporate-Reputation-in-2020_executive-summary_FINAL.pdf).
9 Deloitte (2015) (www2.deloitte.com/content/dam/Deloitte/uk/Documents/corporate-finance/deloitte-uk-corporate-reputation.pdf).
10 ICCO (2020).
11 Game Changers Ipsos (2018).
12 Ocean Tomo (2015) (www.oceantomo.com/intangible-asset-market-value-study/).
13 World Economic Forum (2004) (www.csrwire.com/press_releases/21696-Corporate-Brand-Reputation-Outranks-Financial-Preformance-As-Most-Important-Measure-Of-Success).
14 Bruce (2016) (www.linkedin.com/pulse/brand-reputation-relationship-hidden-intangible-value-stuart-bruce/).
15 Astern (2017).

References

AMO, *What Price Reputation?*, 2019.

Anthony Fitzsimmons and Derek Atkins, *Rethinking Reputational Risk: How to Manage the Risks that can Ruin Your Business, Your Reputation and You*, Kogan Page, 2017.

Brand Finance, *Brand Directory*, 2021 (https://brandirectory.com).

Brand Finance, *Global Intangible Finance Tracker (GIFT)*, 2019 (https://brandirectory.com).

Deloitte, 'Gone in 300 seconds: How corporate reputation influences the value of businesses in the age of social media', 2015 (https://www2 .deloitte.com/content/dam/Deloitte/uk/Documents/corporate -finance/deloitte-uk-corporate-reputation.pdf).

Edelman, *Trust Barometer*, 2020, 2021, 2022.

Fortune, *World's Most Admired Companies*, 2021.

Game Changers Ipsos, *Unlocking the Value of Reputation: The Definitive Link between Corporate Reputation and Better Business Efficiency*, 2018.

ICCO, *World PR Report*, 2020.

Institute of Business Ethics, *Attitudes of the British Public to Business Ethics*, 2020.

Kent Campbell, *Reputation X, Online Reputation Management Statistics*, 2020. Reputation X (see Online Reputation Management Statistics – Reputation Marketing Facts (reputationx.com)).

Ocean Tomo, *Ocean Tomo Intangible Asset Market Value Study*, 2015 (https:// www.oceantomo.com/intangible-asset-market-value-study/).

PRCA, *The Economics of Reputation*, 2014.

Reputation Dividend, *UK Reputation Dividend Report*, 2018.

Stefan Astern, 'Review – Rethinking reputational risk', *Financial Times*, 4 January 2017.

Stuart Bruce, 'Brand, reputation and relationship are the hidden intangible value within companies', *LinkedIn*, 20 May 2016.

The Harris Poll, *Axios Harris Poll 100*, 2021 (https://theharrispoll.com/axios -harrispoll-100/).

The Reputation Institute, *Global RepTrak 100*, 2021.

Weber Shandwick, *The State of Corporate Reputation in 2020: Everything Matters Now*, 2020.

World Economic Forum, *Voice of the Leaders Survey*, 2004.

World Economic Forum, 'Corporate brand reputation outranks financial preformance as most important measure of success', *CSR Wire*, 22 January 2004.

YouGov, *YouGov Brand Index (UK and Ireland)*, 2021 (https://www.brandindex .com).

1

REPUTATION BUILDING

All organisations are the sum of all their parts, and that is as true for a reputation as it is for any other aspect of their operations.

An organisation is not just everything it produces and delivers, but also everything it speaks ... prints ... publishes ... Every word and image produced represents an organisation just as much as a product manufactured or service delivered. Every word and image, internal or external, contributes to a reputation.

But the starting point of a reputation journey has to be information. Without the raw materials at your disposal, you will be unable to make the judgements needed to build, maintain and protect a reputation. So rather than playing it by ear and working from gut instinct, the initial focus has to be on getting behind the details of knowing and under-standing two sets of information:

- Who are your stakeholders?
- What do they think of you?

DOI: 10.4324/9781003293880-2

Once you have this, you can start to put some strategies in place.

Investment decisions would not be made in the absence of data, so why should issues related to reputation be any different?

What makes a reputation?

The simple answer is that it is complicated. A reputation varies between organisations. Each is a unique mix of what it does, what it stands for, what it produces and its people.

Information is the fundamental starting point. This enables leaders to pick apart the layers and get to the building blocks of what their organisation's reputation really is.

An excellent book on reputation management from David Waller and Rupert Younger, *The Reputation Game: The Art of Changing How People See You*, draws a distinction between two types of reputation – character and capability.

Character "reflects moral and social qualities"[1] such as openness, honesty and transparency, while capability reputation reflects "how well you are perceived to be fulfilling a specific task". Reputations for capability are "sticky", but for character they are "much more volatile".

Applying that to some examples seems to bear out this analysis. Why does Volkswagen (VW) continue to sell cars despite having been the subject of one of the biggest corporate scandals of recent years?

The VW emissions scandal in 2015 has been considered "one of the largest corporate scandals of all time".[2] The US Environmental Protection Agency found that VW had installed software in its cars that essentially lowered the emissions of nitrogen compounds when under test conditions. Putting it simplistically, the software helped the cars to cheat the tests and pass them.

Under Waller and Younger's analysis, VW was, to an extent, able to ride out the storm because of its capability – it is known for building quality cars. Whilst the emissions scandal will have damaged that capability, it did not eliminate it.

Part of the damage was down to the way in which the company handled the crisis. Commenting on the VW's approach, Kamal Ahmed, then BBC Business Editor, said: "I think sometimes people forget to be human beings."[3]

But I would go further. VW was at least in part saved from a bigger catastrophe because other companies were also engaged in the same sorts of activities. In the mind of the public, VW was not alone. VW was at the forefront because it was first, but then as other car companies were caught up, the story itself became less interesting, not least to the media.

Despite this, the company, as well as the regulatory authorities, took drastic action. Executives were sent to jail, massive fines were issued, and people lost their jobs. There was a drop in sales and profits, but these have been recovering since the initial scandal. But those who look simply at the share price of a company in the years following a crisis and see little change from the original position are being blinded to many different impacts, not least the short-term disruption. It also ignores the other factors at play in a share price, such as a general economic upturn, and does not compare it with others in the sector who may be doing much better. Innovation may have suffered. Higher wages may be needed to attract talent. Share price alone is a blunt measure in such circumstances.

But the nature of modern companies such as VW is that they own or manage many brands. In the case of VW, the group currently has 12 brands – VW (passenger and commercial), Audi, SEAT, Škoda, Bentley, Bugatti, Lamborghini, Porsche, Ducati, Scania and MAN. This offers a degree of insulation from the fallout of a crisis.

In the aftermath of such a crisis, efforts to rebuild a brand might include mass advertising, sponsorship, celebrity endorsements and influencer marketing, or the other brands owned may be pushed more.

Lesson – The damage inflicted by a crisis is not just measured by share price

---

All this is to say nothing of the ongoing legal disputes and the costs, time and effort, of dealing with the problem. A crisis such as the one delivered by VW's own actions can take decades to finally come to an end. Just think about what the level of profits or share price could have been without the scandal.

But, as many will say, no organisation should ever let a good crisis go to waste. Arguably as a result of "Dieselgate", VW has had to put itself at the forefront of clean vehicle technology. It is not the only firm to take this very seriously, but there is an undoubted added incentive for it, one that also plays to the strength of the firm, of the type identified by Waller and Younger, for capability.

There could be an ironic twist of fate at play here that has forced VW to look more seriously at a different type of future for itself.

Knowing where you are starting

From the very outset, organisations need to be able to answer a number of foundation questions so that they can understand their reputation:

1) Who are your stakeholders?
2) What do they think about you?
3) What do they think about your sector (and "competitors")?
4) What are considered to be the main challenges facing you and the sector?

The answers to questions 2–4 are likely to vary between those audiences identified by the first. They could even be contradictory. The likelihood of emerging from this process with one clear image and plan of action is near zero.

These same questions need to be asked internally as well as externally to provide you with the sort of picture needed to make some strategic decisions.

So, for instance, according to *The State of Corporate Reputation in 2020: Everything Now Matters* by Weber Shandwick, reputation drivers include community relations, industry leadership, ethics and values, corporate culture, training and support for employees, quality of senior leadership other than the CEO or chair, diversity and inclusion in the workplace, governance, environmental responsibility, and philanthropy or charity support.

The reality is that most organisations are not unique. The individuals involved are, but many of the challenges and the issues are common. That means that you, at the very least, need to keep up with the actions of your competitors and recognise that you can also suffer from their reputational fallout.

Consider charities. The number of reputational challenges encountered across the sector has led to a decline in trust for all. The vast majority have had no problems at all, but that does not insulate them.

There are also reputational advantages that can be gained by moving ahead of your competitors, and this can give you kudos with stakeholders. It pays into the "reputation bank".

In an era of emphasis on environmental, social, governance (ESG), which we consider in more detail later, doing more may be a way of moving ahead. But if a competitor moves ahead of you, then you need to play catch-up. Failure to do so will result in a gap. Stakeholders will be disappointed.

There are two critical types of gaps that can emerge and cause reputational damage: the "Competitor Gap", when an organisation consistently fails to achieve the standards achieved by others, and the "Say Do" gap between reality and delivery.

You are only going to know and understand if you face such gaps if you have the information at your fingertips.

Speaking on the Echo Chamber podcast (11 October 2019) about the Total Value Index[4] measure of profit and purpose, Mary Pollard of Portland Communications suggested that "persistent gaps between actual and perceived value are creating reputational risks". The positive impact that businesses generate is, according to Pollard, often undervalued by external audiences. This delivers what they consider to be an "opportunity gap", where businesses can communicate the "Total Value" they deliver to society.

This puts the scenario in a very positive light – an organisation does good, but fails to tell people, or important stakeholders, about it. But in a less positive light, some organisations may over-claim what they do. They stretch just that little too far so that a distance emerges between reality and rhetoric. In simplistic terms, organisations say one thing and then do something else. Both in a positive and negative way, this is often called a "Say Do" gap. Whichever version is in play can lead to reputational challenges.

As with other aspects of reputation management, the gap between reality and rhetoric can only become clear through engagement with stakeholders. The building of the evidence base can occur through face-to-face discussions or through research and measurement.

As Gavin Davis, Managing Partner of Nepean, told me:

> There are multiple tools available to monitor and track reputation but you can't underestimate the importance of actively engaging key stakeholders face-to-face in order to better calibrate automated processes. This requires both empathy and judgement which are skills that cannot be taught and can either be done "old school" by meeting and talking (to media, government etc.) or through focus groups and research with a broader population. I worry that too many organisations simply place their faith in what they are picking up through monitoring or listening tools.

So active engagement with the stakeholders helps to give the "human touch" that information generally demands as well.

It may become clear that you are either benefiting or suffering because of the gap:

- Benefiting if the rhetoric outstrips the reality.
- Suffering if the reality exceeds the rhetoric.

Both scenarios can prove dangerous, although the timescales differ:

- Benefiting if the rhetoric outstrips the reality – immediate benefits, but runs a risk over time when the gap is exposed.
- Suffering if the reality exceeds the rhetoric – insufficient benefits being accrued now, but with the opportunity to address it.

Both scenarios require attention:

- Benefiting if the rhetoric outstrips the reality – devote attention internally to rectifying the gap. This could mean anything from improving employee relations through to better management of the supply chain.
- Suffering if the reality exceeds the rhetoric – devote attention externally to rectifying the gap. This often means improving your communications with stakeholders and being better able to get your side of the story across. It often means you are doing all the right things, but haven't been very good at telling your audiences about them.

It is the evidence base in both cases that means you can identify the problem and then plan actions to address it. One scenario is not necessarily better than the other, because both carry with them risk and require attention. The most important aspect for any leadership team is to have all the information needed so that remedial action can be taken.

Sometimes it is clear to leaders that they are, in effect, over-claiming what they are doing. This is a very easy trap to fall into, especially when under external pressure from, say, the media or politicians. The easiest response is to over-state achievements so that the critics back off. That will provide some immediate, welcome relief, but will not work in the longer term.

Once the real position has been established, then the pressure will only come back, and tenfold. The real position can come to light because of the high levels of disclosure required, but there is always the chance of a whistle-blower or leaks. The best stance to adopt is that the real situation will always become public in the end, and it is only a matter of time. Always be aware of the dangers of a short-term fix when you strongly suspect that it will not stand up to scrutiny. As the cliché goes, "the cover-up is always worse than the crime", and in reputational terms, that is undoubtedly the case.

Lesson – Reputation gaps need to be guarded against

In most instances, the spotlight comes not from leaked information, but from the gap between public pronouncements and actual activity or behaviour. So public statements – social media posts, media statements, annual reports, speeches by executives, interviews etc. – all need to be given a reality check. Can you and the team, hand on heart, stand by every public statement? If the answer is "no" or even "I am not sure", then there is a possible "Say Do" gap. This has nothing to do with stakeholder perceptions, but is simply a case of delivery against statements.

The reality is that management can sometimes become detached from the rest of the organisation and ignorant about what is actually taking place. When that happens, the danger of a "Say Do" gap increases. To avoid a "Say Do" gap developing requires consideration of an organisation's ethics, internal communications and feedback loops. If the right processes are not in place, then there is a real risk that a gap exists without leadership knowing it. However, in some more unethical scenarios, leadership teams may not be too displeased. That is playing fast and loose with their reputation.

The more that stakeholders consider you do not have control, the worse the implications will be. Just think about the position social media companies find themselves in. You can map out a very clear timeline in the case of Facebook, for instance. At the end of 2016, Mark Zuckerberg denied that "fake news" was an issue, especially in the election of Donald Trump as US President:

> Of all the content on Facebook, more than 99% of what people see is authentic. Only a very small amount is fake news and hoaxes. The hoaxes that do exist are not limited to one partisan view, or even to politics. Overall, this makes it extremely unlikely hoaxes changed the outcome of this election in one direction or the other.[5]

Since then, the company has undertaken numerous, often very public, steps to rectify the problem of "fake news".

Why the apparent change of heart, or at least difference in emphasis? One could easily point to the ongoing media, political and activist attention given to the issue. In very simple terms, Facebook has no choice but to take action. Otherwise, it faces the real, and growing, prospect of direct intervention in its activities.

Lesson – Consider the type of information you need to help you make decisions

---

The information challenge

I discussed the importance of evidence in the development of reputation management strategies with Andrew Hawkins, former Chairman of Savanta ComRes.

For Andrew:

> too many organisations simply don't know enough about their reputation and the impact it is having on their bottom line. For

commercial organisations this is a financial one, but in the Not For Profit (NFP) sector it can include wider perceptions of their underlying integrity which then have an impact on areas like fundraising and winning service delivery contracts. The first thing is that organisations must know how they are seen by their stakeholder universe, in order to know whether there are areas of weakness/ strength so that decisions can be taken in the light of all relevant information. It is incredible how many organisations fall at this first hurdle.

The second aspect that organisations typically get wrong is where they fail to think through the impact on their reputation of the decisions they are called on to take. Big organisations are not immune to this – just think of the famous British Airways tail-fin U-turn.[6] They are more likely though to get decisions wrong when they are under time or other pressures, and especially at times of crisis.

Third, organisations too often fail to understand between reputation and linkages between different audiences. This is a risk especially when it comes to workforces: it took just 100 out of Microsoft's 144,000 worldwide employees cause chaos by objecting to Microsoft working with the US Government on a contract for Immigration and Customs Enforcement. Similarly, Shell's problems over the Ogoni people in Nigeria spilled over to become an investor relations issue. All audiences are interconnected. Oxfam's problems over the behaviour of some of their senior staff in Haiti spilled across to become a huge problem spanning public affairs, employee communications and fundraising.

The idea of a "ripple effect" between stakeholders is one to keep in mind at all times. They cannot be managed in isolation. The reality is that the audiences talk to one another, are influenced by one another and listen to one another. Having a poor reputation with one audience can soon bleed into the relationship with another.

For Andrew:

reputation is not only what people think of you directly but also what people think other people think of you. An organisation can fall out of fashion very quickly. Measuring reputations needs to be done:

- *Among all relevant audiences*; for many organisations this will include customers, funders, policy-makers, employees, and possibly suppliers.
- *Regularly*, at appropriate intervals.
- *Comprehensively*, to understand the direction and speed of travel in the "right" direction; it should include asking not only "what do you think of us?" but also "what do other people say about us?" and "do you think we're going in the right direction?"

When it comes to the initial types of questions that should be posed to stakeholders, he considers:

> the standard, if unimaginative, set of questions are around favourability and familiarity but for many organisations of any scale these offer little actionable insight. Rather, the process of measuring reputations is an opportunity to really get under the skin of the audiences that can influence its destiny as well as to crowdsource how an organisation can position itself for future success. So, instead of *only* asking MPs what they think of an organisation, you should be asking what other MPs say about you. Similarly, instead of asking only whether MPs support or oppose a particular regulatory or other development, ask them whether they think a particular outcome is likely or unlikely. It is no exaggeration to say that most organisations are woefully unambitious in planning their reputation measurement.

The strategic insight agency Opinium created the Most Connected Brands Index to help businesses and brands understand how they are connecting with consumers and provide them with ways to improve. From the perspective of reputation management, it is an example of not just measurement, but also its practical application, what steps are required to make the most of the connections and address any weaknesses. I spoke to Steve Looney, Research Director at Opinium, about the Index and its findings. According to Steve:

> It is clear when you look at the Index that being connected is clearly good for business with some of the most successful brands rating highly on our list.

A brand like Netflix is an interesting example, which has seen the strength of connection grow hugely in recent years. Originally launched as a DVD renting service Netflix has evolved and adapted with technology and consumer demand to maintain and build consumer connection by meeting those changing needs.

However, reputation tends to involve wider/different issues, and yes, can help build a connection, but are perhaps a little broader in terms of scope. Issues such as corporate and social responsibility, how employees are treated, the governance of the business etc. are all factors that combine to make a reputation but don't necessarily help make connections. Some obviously can play more of a role: brands like the Co-op, Nationwide and the Body Shop have used more reputational elements to help them make their connection with consumers. So yes, reputation can affect connection, but it's not a given.

The critical element for reputation management is how brands go about building their connections with consumers. A look at the Most Connected Brands Index demonstrates that to good effect:

Amazon is the number one brand and builds connection in many ways with many different types of consumers, from a retail point of view it is the "Everything store" providing everything to anybody, but beyond that it now has Amazon Prime Video delivering content to the next generation of consumers in the format they demand it. The slickness and logistical prowess that Amazon gives consumers talks directly to the "want it now" society that we now live in.

Our top ten also includes brands like Cadbury, Walkers and Heinz, some fantastic FMCG (fast-moving consumer goods) brands that have been around for decades and build their connection in different ways than the new tech giants. These are brands that we all grew up with, and barring disasters, future generations will as well. These brands are based on strong emotional connection providing comfort and security, giving high-quality products time and time again, you can rely on these brands to always be there for you. But they have to keep innovating, all of the three brands have added new lines to their ranges to meet modern trends, being a heritage brand does not guarantee you consumer connection.

Being connected also appears to provide advantages when dealing with stakeholders:

> Strong connections do buy brands more leeway, so stakeholders are more likely to forgive a brand for minor discrepancies if they are invested and have a relationship. If they don't, then they tend to view things in more absolutes, which can be bad news for brands.
>
> A strong connection will also allow brands to ask consumers to make a bigger leap of faith. Virgin is a great example of this, one of the few brands that make the top 100 connected brands that we can't classify into a category. The brand is highly diverse and can do this as it has more bandwidth to do so due to some of the strong connections it made with consumers.
>
> Steve Looney appreciates that there are lots of differing methodologies available, but the others didn't ask questions directly of consumers themselves. He explained that they wanted to create an Index based on the brands that consumers are thinking about, talking about and spending their money on.

In Steve's words, the key metrics of the Index are:

- Prominence – the brands' presence and scale – are you going to drive connection by being the brand that consumers think of first when they think of your category?
- Distinction – the brand's unique identity and ability to set trends – are you going to be the brand that zigs when everyone else zags? Do you genuinely offer something different or perhaps position yourself in a very different way from your competitors?
- Emotion – building that emotional relationship with consumers – this really needs consistency and commitment, as this type of connection is not built overnight.
- Dynamism – the brand's momentum and social traction – how active as a brand are you going to be? How are you going to engage?

The Index also includes a range of "diagnostic measures" which help to "understand brand performance and what drives the most successful brands to the very top, such as social responsibility, value for money and customer satisfaction".

I was particularly interested in the lessons from the Index about how organisations can be better connected? Steve believes that for newer brands, "it's all about finding their niche in the market and exploiting that to develop their connection".

But the real challenge is ensuring that "the connections you build need to be genuine and sustainable – don't make a massive push on social media if you are not going to sustain it, as in the long run that will backfire on the brand".

He believes that the route to better connection is quite simple: "listen to consumers":

> Brands often get caught up in their own self-importance and trans-
> mit a lot but don't always take the time to listen. Building connec-
> tion takes two parties, if you don't listen to how people are feeling
> or what they are thinking about, then you'll never be able to make
> that connection.

That, I would argue, is the same for all audiences. Without the ability to form a connection through listening and learning, you can never improve your reputation with them.

Lindsey Annable, Director of Free Spirit Consulting, believes that "a good brand reputation contributes to differentiation in the marketplace. Businesses need to be familiar with that point of differentiation and keep driving it through all communications. They need to understand whether that communication is successful or not".

This brings her to the need to get the monitoring processes in place:

> Consistency of monitoring is key in order to pick up and respond
> to fluctuations in brand reputation. Given the speed of change of
> opinion it is critical to keep on top of what people are saying about
> your brand. Consistent measures will create benchmarks against
> which deviations are clearer.

That makes it important to ensure that the monitoring is undertaken regularly:

It is about looking out for positive and negative social media mentions or assessing the perception of your brand on a regular basis. Setting up regular monitoring will facilitate observation of trends in your brand performance, sudden dips or unexplained hikes.

Then you can take action, if necessary.

It is this turning of good research into practical action that is the most important aspect of any analysis. Lindsey believes:

> the key to turning research into practical actions is to ensure there are processes in place to take forward the learning from any particular project. This is because any research project can only go so far in making recommendations. As embedded any agency might be in the day-to-day of your organisation, they are not in it full-time. Nor are they party to the many different cogs that make an organisation run, especially the larger it is.

She suggests that it can be helpful to focus the learning around a number of key questions:

- What were the surprises?
- What do we want to take forward?
- How will we do this (who/when)?
- What was interesting, but we are not sure what to do with it? (Whilst this question essentially seems to lack focus, seemingly random ideas can be rich sources of inspiration for, e.g., innovation and working practices.)

Lesson – Listen to and learn from your stakeholders

Ben Lloyd, Deputy Managing Director of Populus, considers that there are a number of issues that organisations typically get wrong when thinking about managing their reputations. The first is related to the failure to appreciate its contribution to business value:

> *Everyone* knows they want a good reputation, but why? Because they don't want a bad one? More need to realise that a good reputation

has consequences. Increased business, lower costs, greater staff retention, less scrutiny from regulators (and the associated time costs), etc. These can all be attributed to a good reputation but you need to know what the drivers are. Just being seen as "a good company" is not enough. What are the drivers of "good", and how do you compare to your competition?

Another failing is related to organisations having a number of reputations:

Very often they think they have only one reputation – they don't. Each audience – friend or foe – has different expectations of you and therefore base their view of your reputation on what matters to them. To only consider the public's view is to ignore how you are seen as a reputable company to invest in. To focus only on financial success is to ignore the potential unethical ways that money is made and what pressure groups might think of that. To know each of these reputations provides a map and a trade-off tool. You know you are going to annoy someone with announcement, best that you know who and the potential impact of that damage.

Others simply "trust instinct too much". Organisations:

need an honest reflection of how they are doing. A critical friend that points out the risks and rationalises their strengths. It is not acceptable for CEOs not to know what their reputational weaknesses are – not acceptable. Even if you think you know – prove it. Understand it. Compare it. Rationalise it. And most importantly, know how not to get caught out by it. Too many see reputation as a consequence not as an opportunity.

Ben highlights the need for organisations to know their audiences – "all of them", as he stresses – and then "know which ones matter and why". He adds that it is best to "be specific, know how to articulate your reputation and why it matters, to staff, to investors, to suppliers. Know how it is a virtue and the advantages that come with it."

For Ben, when gathering your evidence about reputation, you should not rely on one method:

Large-scale quantitative studies will work for populous audiences – large customer bases etc. You can do robust driver analysis to work out what really matters and why. But you cannot apply the same approach with more niche stakeholders. For example, as distinct groups, relevant politicians, journalists, NGOs etc. don't exist in large enough groups to be able to research quantitatively – even if they did, you wouldn't get the richness of their knowledge by doing so. They are experts with a wealth of relevant insight and opinion that you want to hear. Talk to them. Find out what they think and why. Well planned, thoughtful, independent stakeholder research will give you a degree of understanding about your business that you will not get from anywhere else. A view of your reputation that is based on well-crafted, appropriate research will provide a repu-tation roadmap for navigating tough business decisions but also working out what the consequences are likely to be too.

When it comes to the types of questions that you should be asking stake-holders, he suggests trying to get to the heart of the worst-case scenario:

Dig the dirt (sensibly), find out how much better others are. Know what is costing you. But understand the specifics of what you have to do to put it right. Drill down. Know if you have the permission to own a specific reputation space. Are you credible? If not, why not? How do you address it? And beyond the here and now, you need to understand what is over the horizon. What are the trends that are going to set the context for how your reputation is viewed in the future? You need to know them now.

Maintaining an active watch on reputations both internally and exter-nally stems from the actions adopted:

You've identified what matters, now you have to make sure you are bringing about positive change. This could be simple metrics such as number of enquiries, NPS scores, average spend, complaints etc. Some may be more subtle such as favourable trading terms, "benefit of the doubt", preferred supplier status etc. Use the met-rics to hand to keep an eye on them, but make sure they are aligned with your business goals. If they aren't, stop! This is not a vanity exercise.

Invariably, according to Ben, there will be an element of going back to stakeholders to speak to them and "understand how their view of you is changing and the benefits that come with them. That is a reputation building action in its own right".

Technology, too, is always helping to push our understanding forward. We can gain greater and more in-depth understanding of stakeholders as the technology continues to improve. Artificial intelligence (AI) is even making its way into monitoring systems.

According to the team at Signal AI, one of the world's fastest-growing applied AI companies:

> "Revolutionising" seems too often used for how technology impacts a sector or an industry. But with media monitoring, the application of AI has really changed the game.
>
> Traditional methods for monitoring the media were slow, costly and relied on metrics that failed to show the true impact of PR [public relations], like advertising value equivalent, or AVE. For businesses, this meant more time spent on tactical activities as content was produced by more and more people and at a great cost.
>
> To search for the coverage important to you and your business meant using inefficient Google alerts, taking up too much time and providing sometimes irrelevant information, or using Boolean searches. These take time to maintain to show the right results and a knowledge of how Boolean works, something most PRs don't have, for obvious reasons.
>
> AI has simplified the process by providing teams with quick and easy access to how the world's media reacts to a story, as the story is unfolding, in any language, in real time. AI searches for entities, a collection of terms related to the word you're looking for – for example, by analysing how people write or speak about entities, the technology recognises that Apple iPhones cannot be eaten, and apples are not touchscreen. Context is key here.
>
> This means less time spent trawling through individual media outlets, websites or Google alerts. It means receiving relevant in-the-moment results, and it also means PR teams have access to

insights based on data they previously wouldn't have had the time to collect.

You have the ability to search for relevant results over time and around multiple topics. For example, you could see how your company performs in the media around sustainability, or ESG, compare that to the performance of competitors and see where you're excelling or falling short, and make updates to your business strategy accordingly. Using AI here really starts to help augment decision-making by providing time-critical information when you need it.

The other huge advantage of applying AI is around sentiment analysis. The limits of traditional media monitoring meant a focus on volume. AI allows you to see the context behind coverage. Is this a positive or negative story? Looking further outside your trade press, how was the news received by wider society, in different regions and languages.

AI initially saves time and money for communications leaders and PR teams, as it's self-maintaining and provides relevant results in real time. But it also allows teams to reinvest that time into applying and sharing these actionable insights, enabling more strategic decision-making delivering a greater impact to the business.

The claims for such technology are impressive, and it is increasingly available to everyone considering reputations.

The stakeholder challenge

The list of stakeholders relevant to any organisation can be substantial. In the basic sense, a stakeholder is anyone relevant to the running of the organisation.

The importance of insight cannot be questioned.

To get the information that is most useful to you means (a) understanding who your stakeholders are and (b) asking them the right sorts of questions, tailored to them.

Understanding who your stakeholders are is an exercise in itself. No one group within an organisation will have sight of the complete range of stakeholders. Instead, the information needs to be drawn from across the whole organisation.

There will also be an existing base of stakeholder contacts and networks to draw upon. It is extremely rare that no outreach to these groups or individuals has taken place, even informally.

Typically, stakeholders will vary across types of organisations. For instance:

Private company	Public sector/local authority	Charity	Education
Staff	Staff	Staff	Staff
Investors	Local communities	Donors	Students
Shareholders	Voters	Volunteers	Parents/carers
Political	Political	Political	Political
Regulators	Regulators	Regulators	Regulators
Customers	Suppliers	Customers	Suppliers
Suppliers	Media	Suppliers	Funders (public, private, research)
Local communities		Service users	Media
Media		Celebrity supporters	
		Funders (public and private)	
		Media	

This brief and far from exhaustive list illustrates that many of the audiences are the same between different types of organisations. What can be very different is the level of importance they carry. This can vary depending on the issue being considered as well.

Another important factor within the identified groups is taking the time to drill down to the important individuals as well: those who lead the groups, act as spokespeople etc.

In addition to this, consideration also needs to be given to the internal decision-making process for each type of organisation – boards, advisers, trustees, governors, committees and, in the case of some public sector bodies, politicians as well. All are critical stakeholders.

> *Lesson – Stakeholders are not static, stakeholder views are not static*

The reality is that you could enjoy a very strong reputation with some stakeholder audiences, but not others. You will have to focus your efforts on the groups that matter most and/or those that really do not understand you. As you become successful, the stakeholder focus may change.

However you gather your information – polling and research companies, informal feedback etc. – be prepared to undertake this on a rolling or periodic basis. In other words, do not commission a single report and think that it is sufficient.

Rather, you need to keep your eyes and ears open at all times. It is simply impossible to react if you are not paying attention or are relying on out-of-date information.

The danger is that the longer any "Say Do" gap exists, the more likely it is to bleed between stakeholders because they often have interactions with one another. They listen to each other. That could work in your favour, but equally, it could work against you.

Sadly, negative perceptions generally spread more quickly than positive ones. That may be down to the force with which they are delivered. Champions, speaking up on behalf of any organisation, are more difficult to motivate and can be reticent to make public comments. We all know, and have seen examples, of those who are only too happy to attack an organisation.

Lesson – You are not in sole charge of your reputation

Points of intersection between your organisation and those it delivers for, whether they be consumers, clients or service users, are points of both opportunity and danger in terms of reputation. Customer services is not just about solving problems and keeping people happy. It represents an opportunity to build long-lasting relationships and possible champions.

Maintain good relations

Executives often look longingly at the likes of Apple, which effectively uses its reputation to charge a premium for its products. Its customers buy into the whole Apple eco-system and would never dream of buying a product that did not fit within it. The financial markets know that Apple is a good bet and have high expectations of it. Apple is aware of the value of its intangible assets so knows what its customers expect of it and its behaviour.

This is one reason why Tim Cook, Apple CEO, felt compelled to criticise then US President Donald Trump on a range of issues – withdrawing from the Paris Climate Change Accord, his response to the Charlottesville massacre and his attitude to the Dreamers (Deferred Action For Childhood Arrivals), amongst other issues. Cook's key stakeholders, his customers, expected it.

But Cook and Apple also understand the need to have good relationships with the president wherever possible. So presidential visits to production facilities, in effect a sign of their commitment to the president's efforts to re-shore jobs to the US, their membership of the Workforce Policy Advisory Board, and the willingness to meet face-to-face with the president are ways in which they also try to maintain good relations. You can see how even Apple attempts to balance the needs of its, sometimes competing, stakeholders.

Why the need for the good relations? It is clear that presidents have the fate of companies such as Apple in their hands. Their decisions over matters such as tax and tariffs are of fundamental importance. We look in more detail at the role of politics in reputation in Chapter 5.

This can be a difficult and tricky balancing act, but is one that needs to be recognised and addressed.

One way in which the likes of Apple show commitment to a course of action, with whichever stakeholder, is for the full force of the organisation to be behind it. This is clearly backed up by Cook. Strong leadership and a commitment to delivery demonstrate purpose to stakeholders.

Lesson – Reputation needs to be led from the top but is the responsibility of all

---

The perception challenge

Sometimes the perception of a reputation can outstrip the reality. What may start life as a perfectly sensible explanation of the type of organisation you are starts to take on a life of its own. Instead of focusing on what you do well, the story becomes embellished. This is not good PR, it is spin. The facts are vague at best, and designed to mislead at the very worst. Reality is left behind. The further reality is left behind, the bigger the comedown will be when it eventually arrives. And make no mistake, it will arrive.

Perception may come from a number of sources, not least the history of an organisation. That could be positive or a negative. Companies can try to leave their pasts behind them or look to embrace them instead.

But people themselves carry a reputation as well. Individuals can come to represent their organisations. In a negative way, an example of the need to remove a top-level executive who came to represent all that was wrong with the organisation he led was Travis Kalanick, CEO of Uber.

There is no doubting that he helped to take a fledgling start up into a world beater. But this did little to mask a toxic culture for long. A sexual harassment scandal, Kalanick's apparent disparaging attitude towards women, claims of a "bro" culture, footage of him shouting at a driver all added up to give a poor impression of Uber itself. The head had, if you like, infected the body and was threatening its future existence.

But there were also underlying business issues that Uber had failed to address for too long. The business model was questioned by many, then there were continued issues, in many countries, related to driver behaviour and the company's background checks on drivers. Allegations of sexual assaults and rape convictions made the calls for real action louder. Then there were stories of celebrities and politicians being tracked and efforts to undermine a journalist.[7]

Kalanick's eventual departure provided Uber with an opportunity to change fundamentally, and critically, to let key stakeholders know how much it had changed. Such a shift requires a leadership team that is prepared to listen and learn, and as a result, make real and lasting changes. If that includes getting rid of people who are "guilty" of poor behaviour or will not sign up to the new regime, then they need to be out.

The idea that you simply change an executive and everything will come right is very far from the case. Change has to be systemic and for the long term. Stakeholders, especially politicians, are not easily convinced, and the stain of poor behaviour takes time to be removed. There is no "Instant Stain Removal" product available for reputations.

Throughout all of this, Uber could at least rely on a large groundswell of public popularity and wide use of its services. Even in the very worst of times, its customer base was loyal and growing.

But the company has continued to have regulatory issues, not least in its ongoing problems in operating in London. London isn't alone in having issues with Uber, but it remains one of the most high-profile battles. The regulatory authority Transport for London (TfL) has taken action against the firm largely because of its failure to protect passengers. When a "ban" was first announced, Uber was quick off the mark to motivate users of services to try and exert pressure on TfL and the Mayor of London through an online petition which ended up with over 800,000 signatures. Uber was then given a period of time to sort out the failings as TfL perceived them.

During this time, Uber took drastic action to try to rebuild its reputation. Its ads, for example, featured the wide range of safety measures being implemented. Efforts were made to engage with the wider business community. When the new CEO, Dara Khosrowshahi, took over, one of his first moves was to visit London and meet with TfL. This was a very visible break with the attitudes and approach of the past, the Kalanick era. But none of this stopped a "ban" being imposed despite the time allowed for improvements.

In this, and similar cases, stakeholders look for evidence of change. The real power, however, sits with the regulatory authorities, which need fully detailed evidence. This is an example of needing to understand the motivations of stakeholders, but also the nature of their decision-making process.

Lesson – Do the basics right, consistently

We can see potential reputational value in CEOs moving between organisations. The appointment of a new leader can make a positive impact, just as securing the removal of a poorly performing one can.

According to Andrew Hawkins:

> they (organisations) need to be ruthless in assessing the impact of different groups and individuals on their bottom line. It can be

tricky to assess which stakeholders are more important than others but many organisations will use the concentric ring model of stakeholder mapping whereby individuals and audiences nearer the centre are more important than those in the outer circles. If an audience or individual has literally no influence over your regulator or operating environment then don't worry too much about them.

There are other models of stakeholder mapping available, and some try to assign actual numbers. But it is important that stakeholder lists are kept regularly updated and reflect changing circumstances – new issues, sectoral changes, changes in government etc. All of these can change the relative importance or influence of a stakeholder. This, in turn, may mean that specific action is required. Discussing this aspect with Andrew, he said:

Having provided clients with reputation insight over several decades, it is striking to see how many organisations commission reputation research which then gets filed away until the next crisis means it gets taken seriously again. That is the practice of the worst players. The best ones will tie their insight gathering into the strategic plans of the organisation, with a cycle comprising insight, leading to planning, leading to action, leading to insight. It all must be underpinned with measurable objectives to maintain or enhance reputation metrics so that teams can be held to account for achieving them.

This is the type of virtuous cycle that organisations should seek to put in place, rather than a series of random, often haphazard, engagements with long-standing stakeholder allies, which exemplify everything that can be wrong about stakeholder engagement.

Andrew suggests:

organisations should be tracking internal and external measures regularly and probably six-monthly. A typical cycle would involve one annual comprehensive tracking wave with a more modest wave six months later. The major organisational responses will be enacted after the annual comprehensive wave, with adjustments made if necessary six months later.

He also wisely adds that "wherever possible organisations should avoid feeding conflicts of interest and find a way to separate out the advice they get from the measurement of its impact".

Reputation by association

A survey of European association leaders and members by Ellwood Atfield suggested that one of the key jobs of a membership association is to improve the reputation of the sector.[8] It also found that 96% believed that a sector's reputation is either important (22%) or very important (74%) in achieving favourable policy outcomes.

This provides us with an appreciation that to have policy influence needs a good reputation, and that your reputation is, at least in part, related to those around you.

Taking the opposite perspective, what right-minded politician would want to be closely associated with an organisation or a sector with a poor reputation? Where are the votes in that for them? What government would want to defend an organisation or sector with a poor reputation? Surely that is an argument for government intervention? This is a theme we will return to in Chapter 5.

Organisations that wish to have more effect in policy-making need to spend time on their reputations. Just consider the turnaround in the fortunes of social media and tech companies. From being the darling of politicians, they will now be on the receiving end of regulation and taxation. The fall from grace of the big tech giants has been meteoric.

Let's briefly consider some of the changes in position that Facebook has adopted to try to regain the reputational initiative. Having first argued that there was no real problem for it to address related to harmful content, CEO Mark Zuckerberg moved to saying that:

"It's impossible to remove all harmful content from the Internet, but when people use dozens of different sharing services – all with their own policies and processes – we need a more standardized approach."[9]

This has started to shift the debate away from "we don't need regulation" to a potentially complicated, or near impossible, task of designing regulation that can be applied to "dozens of different sharing services". Each service has its own characteristics and challenges, especially when it comes to content, so agreeing on a "'standardized approach" between platforms and between countries is a tall order, to put it mildly.

This new approach, with Facebook trying to be at the vanguard, allows it to try to set the terms for the debate. Its *Charting a Way Forward* document sets out the nature of the challenge, poses questions to help move the debate forward and then proposes guidelines for any regulation.[10]

This came around a year after Zuckerberg called for regulation in four areas – elections, harmful content, privacy and data portability – in an online editorial for the *Washington Post* and on his own Facebook page. He sounded completely contrite when saying: "I believe good regulation may hurt Facebook's business in the near term but it will be better for everyone, including us, over the long term".[11]

A more sceptical person could point to Facebook's failures to protect personal data or adequately deal with the Cambridge Analytica scandal.[12] By suggesting "we are all in this together", Facebook can ensure that it is not singled out for any special attention, which could, in turn, do it harm economically.

Another similarly tricky issue for many tech companies has been how much tax they should pay. Zuckerberg believes that "tech companies should serve society" and, to that end, Facebook supports the Organisation for Economic Co-operation and Development (OECD) initiative to create fair global tax rules coming out of the digitisation of the economy.

Again, Facebook is seen to be doing exactly the right thing in calling for the tax situation to be sorted out, but whether the OECD initiative is likely to come up with workable and deliverable plans anytime soon is more disputable.

> *Lesson – No one is immune, even the biggest can fail reputational challenges*

The media is littered with business relationships that come to an end, not just because of the fear of reputational damage, but because the association sends out contradictory messages or undermines the values or ethics of an organisation. Quite simply, the fit just doesn't work anymore.

Take this tweet from Greg Glassman, CEO of CrossFit. In response to a tweet from the Institute of Health Metrics and Evaluation stating that "Racism and discrimination are critical public health issues that demand an urgent response. #BlackLivesMatter",[13] Glassman replied saying, "Its FLOYD-19", apparently attempting to draw a "humorous" comparison between the lockdowns introduced as a result of COVID-19 and the death at the hands of police officers in Minneapolis of George Floyd.[14]

There was an apology and a commitment that Glassman, CrossFit HQ and the CrossFit community "will not stand for racism".[15] The apology, across a series of tweets, went out on the corporate CrossFit account, not Glassman's own account on which the original tweet was posted.

But there was also an email, according to the media, in which Glassman responded to a company affiliate asking for a statement on the death of George Floyd in a dismissive and insulting way.

As a direct result, affiliate gyms removed the CrossFit name and Reebok announced that it was ending its relationship with the company.

Glassman continued to be accused of racism despite the words of the apology. Within weeks, Glassman had to sell the company. The new owner's first statement? "Racism and sexism are abhorrent and will not be tolerated in CrossFit".[16]

When organisations have to deal with issues of relationships, they have several options:

1) Stick together – they may be happy with the relationship and believe that the potential damage is being overplayed, the adverse attention will be short-lived or that there is more to be gained through showing loyalty. That can strengthen the relationship which may bring with it more benefits over the long term. This needs to be balanced against the attention that will doubtless come with sticking together.

2) Review the relationship – that would buy time to make a final decision and would allow any apologies made or promised changes in behaviour to be expressed. This needs to be balanced against the perception of a lack of clear action and delay. There is always the danger that you end the relationship as a result of the review, but receive none of the kudos for making a swift initial decision.

3) End the relationship – a quick decision would demonstrate leadership, but potentially a lack of loyalty, especially if the problem is nuanced.

Of course, all these courses of action are a case of balance. But when any of the actions of any supplier or commercial partner are so much the antithesis of your own standards, values and ethos, then where is the upside of sticking with them?

Questions posed to organisations in a crisis are often highly simplistic and do not reflect the entire picture of what has taken place. But unless an organisation can explain itself in equally simple terms, then it needs to be prepared for sustained pressure on the issue.

Changes often need to be made after any crisis. If everything was working perfectly, then a crisis would never have arisen in the first place. Some organisations will promise an independent inquiry as a way of reassuring stakeholders and solving the problem. Any genuinely independent review will want to take a deep dive into everything from the behaviour of staff through to timelines, reporting structures, documents and procedures.

An independent inquiry will also want free rein to say what has gone wrong and make recommendations about what changes are required. These changes, the solutions to the problem, need to be based on insight and a determination to secure change. Anything more superficial, or less independent, will simply fail.

That makes the adoption of the proposed solutions pretty much fundamental. To outsource the review and then ignore its findings would be to play Russian roulette with a reputation. This is especially the case when the initial crisis has had a high profile. Ignoring the solutions would be enough of a story to get the media interested once again. To ignore the solutions would be a new angle to the story, and would provide the media with all the excuse it needs to revisit the story and keep it going.

The promise of an independent review may be seen by some as a superficial attempt to deflect the media, but it can bring a real benefit. A review can bring a fresh perspective and does not carry potential in-built biases or concerns about existing relationships. This brings with it the confidence needed by senior teams and boards to implement the recommended changes.

Lawyers are often chosen to undertake such reviews. There is never just one reason why, but it includes their ability to unpick complex issues, ask challenging questions, follow evidence wherever it may take them and so on. But, arguably more importantly, they benefit from the very reputation of being a lawyer. It carries with it an air of professionalism and independence. Lawyers also benefit from their own tough regulatory requirements. These cover everything from money laundering through to client conflicts.

That is not to say that such a review simply needs to be put on the board table or desk of a newspaper or news website editor. The presentation of an independent report can and should be considered as well – not as a way of spinning or putting a positive gloss on the findings, but to help provide some context and background. The timings around implementing proposed changes need to presented, and explanation may be required about why some findings are prioritised over others.

So what lessons can be drawn from organisations whose reputations collapse during a crisis?

1) Sometimes a crisis is just so toxic that it supersedes all the good built up over the years. The "capability reputation" simply runs out.
2) If an organisation has "form", in other words it has suffered from previous crises, this means it starts from a lower position and its reputation is already damaged.
3) The actions taken in one place, or country, are no longer isolated there thanks to global media channels.
4) Some crises and allegations are just more toxic than others.
5) If your friends and allies will not stand with you, then no one else will.
6) The more competitive the market in which you operate, the more options there are to defect from you and the more likely it is that criticism from the sector will come your way.

All organisations should think about whether these sorts of factors apply to them.

Where do we go from here?

As we are starting to discover, building a reputation is about more than delivering good news. It is about knowing and understanding stakeholders, their expectations and knowledge. It means being able to address misunderstanding or misinformation. But it also has to mean having the commitment to deal with deficiencies internally.

That is what it means to have a genuine commitment to your reputation.

Notes

1 Waller and Younger (2018), p17.
2 "A Decade of Disruption", *Evening Standard*, 11 December 2019.
3 Quoted in *PR Week*, October 2015.
4 Portland Communications (2020) (https://totalvalueindex.portland-communications.com).
5 Zuckerberg (2016) (www.facebook.com/zuck/posts/10103253901916271).
6 British Airways took the decision to replace its traditional Union flag tail fin with a series of "ethnic" designs, and in the process upset former Prime Minister Margaret Thatcher.
7 For a handy list of Uber scandals, see Levin (2017) (www.theguardian.com/technology/2017/jun/18/uber-travis-kalanick-scandal-pr-disaster-timeline).
8 Dober and Riggins (2018).
9 Bickert (2020) (https://about.fb.com/wp-content/uploads/2020/02/Charting-A-Way-Forward_Online-Content-Regulation-White-Paper-1.pdf).
10 Ibid.
11 Zuckerberg (2020).
12 The scandal involved the harvesting of personal information on Facebook.
13 Institute for Health Metrics and Evaluation (IHME), tweet, 6 June 2020 (https://twitter.com/ihme_uw/status/1269343305147518976).
14 A screenshot of Glassman's tweet can be seen at Pamela Kufahl, "CrossFit's Greg Glassman Apologizes for George Floyd Tweet after Reebok Ends Relationship", *Club Industry*, 8 June 2020 (www.clubindustry.com/commercial-clubs/crossfit-s-greg-glassman-apologizes-for-george-floyd-tweet-after-reebok-ends).
15 CrossFit, tweet, 8 June 2020 (https://twitter.com/crossfit/status/1269802501873623040).
16 Eric Roza, tweet, 24 June 2020 (https://twitter.com/RozaEric/status/1275792231245455362/photo/1).

References

'A decade of disruption', *Evening Standard*, 11 December 2019.

David Waller and Rupert Younger, *The Reputation Game: The Art of Changing How People See You*, Oneworld Publications, 2018.

Echo Chamber Podcast, Interview with Mary Pollard, Portland Communications, 11 October 2019.

Eric Roza, Tweet, 24 June 2020 (https://twitter.com/RozaEric/status /1275792231245455362/photo/1).

John Harrington, 'BBC Business Editor Kamal Ahmed: Volkswagen's problem is it "doesn't speak human"', *PR Week*, 25 September 2015.

Mark Dober and Phil Riggins, 'Reputation by association', Communication Director, 2018.

Mark Zuckerberg, *Facebook blog post*, 13 November 2016.

Mark Zuckerberg, 'Mark Zuckerberg: Big tech needs more regulation', *Financial Times*, 16 February 2020.

Monika Bickert, 'Charting a way forward', *Facebook blog post*, 17 February 2020.

Portland Communications, *Total Value Index*, 2020 (https://totalvalueindex .portland-communications.com).

Sam Levin, 'Uber's scandals, blunders and PR disasters: The full list', *The Guardian*, 28 June 2017.

Weber Shandwick, *The State of Corporate Reputation in 2020: Everything Now Matters*, 2020.

2

GETTING AHEAD OF REPUTATION

There is no one ideal way of building and protecting a reputation. Instead, there are a number of interwoven strands. It is nearly impossible to completely unpick all aspects of a reputation, but it is possible to understand the risks to it and address them.

I consider the development of reputation to have three stages:

1) Building – early stages
   All organisations need an initial period of assessment before awareness raising and letting stakeholders know what you do and what they stand for.
2) Maintaining – the steady state
   This stage is focused on keeping stakeholders informed but also maintaining an awareness of new issues as they arise. This stage is as much about trying to look to the future and taking pre-emptive actions as anything else. A steady state need not be reactive, it can be proactive.

DOI: 10.4324/9781003293880-3

3) Protecting – at times of pressure
   Organisations need to take any actions needed, especially during a crisis, to reassure stakeholders. That may mean taking corrective measures.[1] This stage is more manageable if the previous ones have been followed so that an understanding and trust has been developed by stakeholders.

> *Lesson – Recognise what stage you are at*

As with any decision, always start from the basics. In the case of reputation, the question to ask is who is responsible for it? It might sit with the person responsible for risk management. It might come under communications. The legal director may be responsible, but can you manage reputation solely through the law? As we have already seen, "just" following the law may not be sufficient when it comes to reputation management.

This demonstrates a second fundamental challenge. Does the person responsible have the tools at their disposal to manage a reputation?

Too often the answer is no. The lawyer doesn't control HR. HR may have some element of internal communications with staff, but no external communications role. If communications is "in charge", then it often does not have a seat in the board room so can lack visibility. And so on.

My argument is that no single person can deal with all the strands of reputation, so instead a fruitful approach is for a Chief Executive, or similar, to have overall responsibility for reputation. Why? Because they alone can ensure that all the levers necessary can be utilised. Everyone, ultimately, reports to them.

Without that sort of oversight, gaps will emerge as different parts of an organisation simply deal with that element of reputation that sits with them. Such a siloed approach will ultimately lead to trouble.

The more that any senior leadership sees the value in reputation management, the more they will devote resources to it. The value of reputation has to be demonstrated in a way that resonates with the various needs of a leadership team. That means knowing and understanding what those needs are and putting the values or measures in place which enable effective communication with them; talking the right language and, if needed, showing where efforts have worked well for others. There is nothing like a bit of shaming against competitors or others in the sector to focus attention.

Lesson – Think about who is really in control

Now that you have considered who is in charge, what should the first steps be?

Thinking ahead

We have all witnessed a number of ways in which organisations have failed spectacularly in their responses to COVID-19. The longer-lasting implications have still to be seen, but what is already clear is that "follow-up" reputational damage through new, but related, stories continues. Even if the initial storm passes, the media and politicians have long memories.

The fast fashion company Boohoo has been going through one such crisis played out over a period of weeks and returned to by the media. It brought immediate financial issues as well as longer-term potential political ramifications.

The essence of Boohoo's issue relates to allegations of modern slavery in its supply chain. Following the initial media reports of low pay (£3.50 per hour) and extremely poor and unsafe conditions in factories producing its garments in Leicester, UK, it appointed an independent lawyer to undertake a complete review. According to *The Times*, more than £2 million was taken off the value of the company in the weeks after the news initially broke.[2]

Boohoo realised the severity of the issues involved and the impact on its main stakeholders, younger age group consumers. So along with the independent investigation came a £10 million investment to "eradicate supply chain malpractice" along with speeded-up work with two supply chain auditors. It also sacked suppliers for breaking its already established code of conduct – so clear, immediate and public signs of action.

Almost immediately after the story broke, Next, ASOS, Very and Zalando, which all stock Boohoo products (and the other brands it owns), all stopped selling its goods. There could, of course, be a way back for Boohoo, but it was a clear early sign of the scale of the challenge. It needs to regain the faith of those selling its brands as they too have their reputations to consider.

One of Boohoo's largest investors, Aberdeen Standard Investments, sold 27 million shares after saying about the response to the allegations: "We view their [Boohoo's management team] response as inadequate in scope, timelines and gravity".[3]

Other investors investigated, whilst some brought more shares. There is never one completely clear picture, and different organisations will respond in different ways. Sometimes this may come down to whether they have a public name or consumer base themselves. The way that, for instance, Next responds could well be different from an institutional shareholding company with no household name.

However, concerns had been raised about working conditions in Leicester previously, so questions about why fashion retailers with a supply chain in the city had not taken action would rightly be asked.[4] Even if companies may not have announced anything publicly at the time of these original concerns, for instance if they were not themselves named, an obvious step would be to review the situation, check for weaknesses and then take remedial action, if needed. They would at least subsequently be able to demonstrate that they took action as soon as the issue came to light. That is the sort of behaviour stakeholders want to see and that protects reputations.

The more that organisations are ahead of the game in terms of the expectations on them, the more they will be able to maintain their reputations.

Lesson – Knowledge without action will not be forgiven

The idea that attacks from activists, vested interests or campaigning groups can be completely avoided would be untrue. There will always be challenges and in an open, democratic society that should be welcomed. No organisation should simply be allowed to do what it wants.

Some organisations work closely with those who are likely to challenge them so that the questions are posed behind closed doors in the first place. I first wrote about some of the strategies that activists use to attack companies but also their responses back in 2003, so this is nothing new.[5] Leadership teams need to choose an approach that helps them to keep on top of the moving focus of challenges. One approach may be to work alongside the activist groups or NGOs who can act as critical friends and keep them on the right path.

Others may choose to "outsource" their compliance procedures so that a level of independence is maintained and others, from outside, can more easily scrutinise what the organisation is up to. It allows an organisation to say, "Do not take our word on it, look at this independent assessment". Such assessments can cover everything from employee relations through to supply chain management and the sourcing of materials used in production.

But expectations shift over time. Just consider how organisations look after and share our personal data and how rapidly attitudes have changed about this. From personal data being "a price worth paying" for free services and products, we are now more aware of the value of our data and how organisations have extracted financial returns from them. Then there are single-use plastics. A couple of years ago, few worried about buying a bottle of water and then throwing away the bottle itself. Now many people carry their own carry reusable bottles and some cities have installed drinking water fountains. Outsourced compliance procedures need to be updated to meet current expectations, not those of the past.

Why do such changes happen? There is no single reason. Instead, it often is an accumulation of factors over a period of time. But chief amongst these would be campaigns, and political and media attention. Here, it is always useful to have an appreciation of how campaigning organisations work. If they achieve what they are campaigning for, then they very rarely come to an end. Instead, they will look to build on that achievement and move forward another stage. Campaigns are never static. Public health campaigns do not stop after securing a change such as a sugar tax or plain packaging, instead they look to move on to a new policy target.

The conversations move on and the levels of expectations increase. It is rare for expectations to ever decrease. The need to get economies back and running as quickly as possible after the COVID-19 crisis could lead to a period where businesses in particular are allowed to put priorities other than growth to one side for a period of time. Many environmental campaigners have already expressed such fears, believing that climate change targets could be "paused", with potentially huge ramifications.

Being on top of expectations also means considering your campaign opponents and their positions. It means thinking about how they could seek to attack you and where your points of weakness are. Furthermore, you need to think ahead as well.

Having this level of awareness and understanding about your campaign opponents means:

1) Addressing them internally – if they have hit on a matter that needs addressing, then you need to do your best to rectify the problem. To not do so could look like negligence and offers your reputation no future protection.

2) Addressing them externally – you do not always have to take the criticism lying down. The opponents will not always be right and may not be aware of the latest advances you have made. Sometimes a fightback is entirely the right thing to do, to defend your position. Think back to the point about campaigns often being a progression. If you do cede ground on one point, where does that take the conversation on to? Externally, it could mean more media attention, but it will almost certainly mean political consideration as well. Part of understanding campaigns is recognising where they will be focusing their efforts. It is too easy to take such attention personally, but the reality is that campaigns will target you, your competitors and those in your sector, but also political audiences as well. Why? Because if they can convince those political audiences, then it does not matter what your position is, instead the politicians will pass a law and make you comply.

But your competitors can apply pressure on you as well. Where they take the conversation may leave you with no option but to follow their lead. Their position becomes the standard by which all others are judged. Unless you match them, you run the risk of the market moving away from you. That may mean that you have to think about not only matching them, but exceeding them. In turn, that comes with it the chances of an "arms race", which may suit no one, so always be wary of moves that only serve to accidentally ratchet up the pressure.

This brings a focus on not making rash decisions simply to cope with short-term pressure. Instead, work through the implications.

Lesson – Reputations are not just about you

Advocacy

Much of the value in a reputation is derived from advocacy. That is not just about what you tell stakeholders about your actions, but about responding to the criticism of others as well.

However, advocacy is not just about what you say. It should also be what others say about you and their willingness to defend you and respond on your behalf. There are various terms used for individuals and organisations willing to do this – supporters, advocates, friends, allies, champions.

The stronger the reputation, the more likely your arguments and responses are to be believed.

Arguments and responses that you put forward are not aimed only at replying or counteracting criticism or the views of opponents, but also, in a polite way, undermining their authority on the issue as well – in simple terms, placing a question mark beside their reputation. A weaker reputation on their part damages how much they will be listened to.

According to the Ipsos report *Unlocking the Value of Reputation: The Definitive Link between Corporate Reputation and Better Business Efficiency*, consumers are more likely to see and believe advertising from companies they trust, and then act on it. But turn that around. A weaker reputation damages that impact and puts you at a disadvantage over others.

This is where the development of key messages is critical. These can be delivered in various written forms, in direct engagement, but through interviews as well.

When a new leader comes into an organisation, they will always want to put their own fingerprints on it. But very often a change of leadership is brought about by a crisis. Under those circumstances, a new leader has to:

1) Review the organisation's behaviour that led to the crisis in the first place.
2) Share the findings of any review.
3) Map out a new path for the future.

But critically, this needs to be done in a public way. Why? So that trust and confidence can be rebuilt. Some audiences may need to be talked through the actions being taken in more detail than others. It is essential not to assume that such information is conveyed to them through, for instance, the media. This is where there is no substitute for direct engagement.

The ability to get your side across and to expose yourself to their cross-examination and questions is often part of the answer when building a reputation, but definitely when rebuilding one. It is the time when full exposure to a cleansing light is essential.

The crisis

For many leaders, it is the time of crisis that really brings with it the focus on reputations – personal and organisational.

Andrew Hawkins, former Chairman of Savanta ComRes, believes:

> reputation cannot hide from behaviour; the two should and probably will be the same. If a poorly behaving organisation has a reputation problem, the measures it takes to address it are only ever a

sticking plaster, from behind which its poor behaviour will at some point emerge. On the other hand, when an organisation which behaves with integrity hits a reputation problem, the challenge it faces is one of getting the truth out, not covering it up. That is an altogether far easier and more sustainable task.

Ultimately, organisations whose behaviour falls short of their reputation will fail to meet their ambitions.

Lesson – Reputation management is not crisis management

The success of coping and dealing with a crisis is in part down to past behaviour: 87% of respondents to a survey claimed that they had been through a significant crisis situation that had negatively impacted their business in 2019.[6] On the one hand that is a sign of the consequences of a crisis. Aside from the financial impact, decreased sales etc., one of the often overlooked aspects is the time and internal resources taken to deal with it.

A crisis is often in the eye of the beholder, the ones having to deal with it. The more experience you have of crises, the better you should get at recognising and dealing with them. But 36% of executives in the same survey reported mental health issues as a result of dealing with a crisis.[7]

This finding bears out anecdotal feedback I have received from leaders who have to deal with crises. They draw all the time that you have, and "normal operations" are inevitably put to one side. A crisis takes over not just the working day, but also the rest of a leader's waking hours as well. It literally takes over their lives. No wonder it has an impact on mental health.

Of course, leaders will have different views as to what actually constitutes a crisis. A problem is not always a crisis. There is sometimes an overestimation of the impact of such a problem, because saying that you have successfully dealt with a crisis implies you are an effective leader. It does the ego no harm at all.

However, those in larger organisations sometimes forget that what may, to them, seem like a minor problem would, to a smaller body, represent a major disruption and a significant impact on their operations. But crisis triggers are similar.

In '6 Signs Your Corporate Culture Is a Liability', Sarah Clayton suggests the main factors that account for a majority of cultural risk:

1) Inadequate investment in people.
2) Lack of accountability.
3) Lack of diversity, equity and inclusion.
4) Poor behaviour at the top.
5) High-pressure environment.
6) Unclear ethical standards.

These can all be addressed if a leadership team put their minds to it. Clayton goes on to set out four steps that can be taken to guard against such cultural risk:

1) Secure explicit commitment from the top.
2) Charter a cultural vigilance team.
3) Define (or refresh) your behavioural expectations.
4) Design an ongoing cultural vigilance strategy, and act on it.
5) Weave culture into strategy development and annual planning processes.[8]

There are always choices facing any leader or leadership team, requiring balances and compromises.

What has been particularly noticeable in recent years is how even those who would traditionally have been considered to have a "hard-nosed" approach have been softening. The focus for such companies on simply making money for their shareholders has been replaced with consideration for wider societal concerns whilst, of course, delivering returns.

There is a growing belief that business decisions are being driven by ESG – environmental, social and governance – considerations. Cultural change has been listened to.

Consider how this new culture has impacted BlackRock, the world's largest asset manager. It now states:

Our purpose is to help more and more people experience financial well-being. In pursuit of this, a focus on long-term sustainability is embedded across our business. From integrating environmental, social and governance (ESG) practices into our investment processes to creating positive social impact by serving communities in the UK, we are dedicated to helping clients, employees, shareholders and communities achieve long-term, financial well-being.[9]

Larry Fink, Chairman and Chief Executive Officer of BlackRock, in his 2020 annual letter on corporate governance, was explicit in saying that, for instance: "Climate change has become a defining factor in companies' long-term prospects". He went on to say:

A strong sense of purpose and a commitment to stakeholders helps a company connect more deeply to its customers and adjust to the changing demands of society. Ultimately, purpose is the engine of long-term profitability. ... Given the groundwork we have already laid engaging on disclosure, and the growing investment risks surrounding sustainability, we will be increasingly disposed to vote against management and board directors when companies are not making sufficient progress on sustainability-related disclosures and the business practices and plans underlying them.[10]

Business Roundtable, "an association of chief executive officers of America's leading companies working to promote a thriving U.S. economy and expanded opportunity for all Americans through sound public policy", was founded in 1972. In August 2019, it announced a new "Statement on the Purpose of a Corporation".

The statement set out "a modern standard for corporate responsibility" and covered everything from investing in employees with fair compensation, dealing fairly and ethically with suppliers, supporting communities in which they work, to a commitment to transparency and effective engagement with stakeholders. This was viewed as a significant move, not least because of the high-profile membership of the Roundtable. However, many have pointed to a lack of teeth and enforcement. The headline chosen for the media release on the statement said that the purpose of the corporation was now to promote "An Economy That Serves All Americans".

Whilst the organisation exists to promote US business interests, very many of its members are global operations. Critics will point to the possible conflicts that could exist between "an economy that serves all Americans" and what that could mean for consumers, suppliers or the environment in other parts of the world.

Possibly the greatest threat to this new-style approach contained in the statement is the economic consequences of COVID-19. Can businesses really rebuild themselves and adhere to this new approach, or will we see an emphasis on securing economic returns as quickly as possible? This would have implications for every aspect of operations, from employment through to the environment.

Changing behaviour?

Many organisations have been trying to deal directly with the reputational damage inflicted by failing to deal with climate change. This needs them to be loud and clear in how they are changing their behaviour.

The owner of British Airways, IAG, has committed to achieving net zero carbon emissions by 2050. This made it the first major airline group to make such a commitment.

Starbucks launched a plan to cut its waste, water use and carbon emissions by 2030. Chief Executive Officer Kevin Johnson said: "Our aspiration is to become resource positive – storing more carbon than we emit, eliminating waste, and providing more clean, freshwater than we use".

The public letter setting out the plans included initial targets for 2030, a commitment to being transparent in its reporting, as well as working with stakeholders in the drive.

Arguably the most important measure Starbucks announced was baseline created in partnership with Quantis and the World Wildlife Fund against which future progress will be measured.

The areas of focus to achieve the goals are:

- Expanding "plant-based" menu items.
- Shifting away from single-use to reusable packaging.
- Investing in regenerative agriculture, reforestation, forest conservation and water replenishment in the supply chain.

- Better ways to manage waste.
- More eco-friendly stores, operations, manufacturing and delivery.[11]

Microsoft has promised to be carbon-negative by 2030, so it will remove more carbon from the environment than it emits.

At the start of 2020, JetBlue Airways committed to being carbon-neutral by the July of that year by offsetting their emissions – a target that was hit. The announcement was the first by a large US airline. They aimed to achieve this by offsetting their carbon by investing in projects such as those which protect forests and develop renewable energy.

Rio Tinto signed a deal with China's largest steel maker, China Baowu Steel Group, its biggest partner, to research ways to reduce carbon emissions in the steel industry.

The Motion Picture Association of America has felt compelled to detail what its member studios are doing to help address environmental concerns covering everything from donated meals through to sets saved from landfill.[12] It seems that no sector or industry can now avoid the green spotlight.

"Climate change is a brand safety issue", according to Lou Pakalis, Senior Vice-president of Customer Engagement and Media Investment at Bank of America,[13] and these examples demonstrate that companies have recognised this.

Lesson – Ask if your organisation needs to change its behaviour

---

But an organisation still has to get the basics of its business right. The fallout from Rio Tinto's involvement in the destruction of an ancient Aboriginal site in Western Australia forced the resignation of its Chief Executive, Jean-Sébastien Jacques, and other executives. The reputational fallout has been huge, sparking reaction across the world. From reports, it appears that the company took legal advice before proceeding with the destruction, but failed to consider the communications or reputational implications – to say nothing of the effect felt by the indigenous community.

In 2019, the London Metal Exchange decided that it would only permit responsibly sourced metals to be traded from 2022. The *Financial Times* described the move as "one of the biggest shake-ups in the organisation's history".[14]

The decision appeared to be a response to demands, from consumers and investors alike, for sustainable products. However, it would also provide companies who use metals in their products, such as computers and mobile phones, comfort about the products they are using. This is exactly the type of move that satisfies all parts of the supply chain.

The rules mean that those producers who work out of high-risk areas, often conflict zones, are required to meet international guidelines on responsible sources. Failure to abide by the rules could mean being de-listed from the metals exchange. For the first time, a listing is not just down to the product itself, but how it is sourced as well: "For over a century, the LME has stipulated only metallurgical standards for its brands. And while we do not change our approach lightly, we now believe that the time is right for responsible sourcing principles to be embedded".[15]

Apple was amongst those companies criticised for its use of metals. It announced in 2019 that it was partnering with RESOLVE, an NGO that "forges sustainable solutions to critical social, health, and environmental challenges by creating innovative partnerships where they are least likely and most needed", to source sustainable gold from mines in Alaska, British Columbia and the Yukon. Apple has also continued efforts to recycle the components in iPhones by dissembling them and then reusing materials in new products, MacBook Airs, Minis, in batteries etc. Addressing areas of reputational weakness in the business in such a manner is clearly designed to reassure stakeholders.

Companies, charities and individuals now all need to act in accordance with the general levels of values displayed by society. These are not written down anywhere. They are not just what is codified into law. They do not remain static. Organisations need to maintain constant vigilance, and if values seem to be changing, then they need to reconsider their actions in light of those changes. Consider your actions as being "law plus" – the law (what you need to do) plus (what you should do).

> *Lesson – Values require constant vigilance*

Especially when it comes to paying a "fair share", many organisations seek to minimise the amount of money they pay in tax. Whilst this is in most cases perfectly legal, in the court of reputation management it is increasingly unacceptable. Governments are successfully putting the spotlight on mainly large global tech firms that enjoy massive income yet seemingly pay little tax. For governments that are increasingly struggling to pay for the public sector, especially following COVID-19 – health, education etc. – they feel that they are missing out on income that could go towards paying for these services.

What many companies have now taken to is claiming that governments need to sort out the problem, and that this should preferably be done at a global level.

Whilst this may, in theory, be an ideal scenario, it is unlikely to come to pass in the near future. European-wide agreement can be challenging enough to organise, but then add in the US and you can see the complications. Many of the big tech firms are US-based, and the reaction of then President Trump to proposed taxes by the UK and France illustrates the scale of the challenge. The US threatened tariffs on French goods when France passed a law suggesting a 3% tax on revenue generated from delivering services to French users. The US believed that the law was aimed squarely at US firms. As a result of the pressure, France delayed the implementation of the legislation. The US threatened similar retaliation against the UK for its plans for a digital tax.

The seemingly near-constant attacks on the tech firms for their tax payment arrangements come alongside a range of other issues – a failure to police harmful and abusive content, allowing fake news to percolate etc. – that call into question their ability to take and implement decisive action.

For the politicians, this leaves them with little option but to intervene. For the likes of Facebook, this has led them to suggest that governments need to take a lead on deciding on what harmful content is[16] and an apparent willingness to pay more tax if a global lead is taken.[17]

On one level, this is an appreciation that these big and difficult decisions are not for private companies, especially large companies, to decide. They are issues that need to be agreed between democratically elected governments reflecting the needs and wishes of the people they represent.

On another level, by shifting responsibility onto global bodies, companies such as Facebook are at least partly delaying the chances of action being taken and also increasing the opportunity for the lowest common denominator to be adopted. In other words, the only actions that can be agreed are the least disruptive ones that will have the least impact on the companies themselves. They are also able to shift the reputational damage onto government and politicians. These sorts of announcements by organisations should always be seen through the prism of reputation management.

What Zuckerberg and others are clearly trying to do is remove their own culpability for when things go wrong in the future. Instead of then being the responsibility of the individual company, it becomes the fault of indecisive governments. The companies "are doing all they can", whilst governments are failing to agree actions.

Such an approach is not without its risks. Campaigning groups and activists will continue to highlight what they see as poor practice. However, it could buy organisations some more time so that they can tighten up, improve their own practices and learn from others.

Lesson – Always be prepared to learn from others

The issue of tax is a clear example of business decisions, risks analyses and public comments all coming together to impact on reputation. If any one of these aspects is not given due consideration, then damage will result.

It is important to track the way that stakeholders feel about critical issues such as tax. The way to track change is to pay attention to what stakeholders believe. Political questions, media coverage, online sentiment etc. are always useful sources.

Fulfilling legal requirements can be seen as the minimum expected. The real challenge is for an organisation to push and challenge itself to identify the next area of improvement. This has to be in line with its values, but such anticipation opens a space to improve reputations and, more selfishly, gain an advantage over others.

Monitoring progress

According to the first Global Consumer Survey by the Programme for the Endorsement of Forest Certification (PEFC), more than 80% of consumers want brands to use labels on products to tell them about their responsible sourcing. The same research found that 54% said that certification labels are the strongest proof that environmental and sustainable practices have been considered.[18]

Early adopters of a certification scheme can use it as an opportunity to differentiate themselves from their competitors. But some companies have gone further, building their whole reputation on their ethical status.

For this to work, any organisation has to constantly police the certificate as well. Signing up is the starting point. Maintaining a constant watch is the next. You cannot fully outsource responsibility.

Take Tesco as an example. In December 2019, it suspended production at a factory in China which was producing Christmas cards and also stopped selling them. Why? The media reported that when a customer opened one of the cards, they found a message asking for help. The message read: "We are foreign prisoners in Shanghai Qinqpu prison China. Forced to work against our will. Please help us and notify human rights organization."[19]

Tesco's response rightly focused on its shock at the allegation, and went on to say:

> We have a comprehensive auditing system in place and this supplier was independently audited as recently as last month and no evidence was found to suggest they had broken our rule banning the use of prison labour. If a supplier breaches these rules, we will immediately and permanently de-list them.[20]

This gets to the very heart of the issue for organisations: they need to police whatever certification processes they have in place. In other words, they need to police the police.

This can even happen to those organizations which look carefully at their supply chains because they understand how fundamental they are to their reputations. They are not immune from issues. IKEA has been accused of using wood from illegally felled beech trees in its products. This goes against the very sustainability policy that the company features prominently:

> Because wood is so important to IKEA, we work together with FSC [Forest Stewardship Council] to take care of the world's forests. Through responsible forest management, we make sure we have forests for all, forever. By the end of 2020, we aim for all our wood to come from more sustainable sources including FSC certified and recycled wood.

The allegation was not that IKEA was deliberately using this wood, but that the FSC certification process it used was flawed. IKEA's response was: "We have initiated an independent audit of our wood supply chain in Ukraine. We have also asked Assurance Services International (ASI) – who are FSC's independent auditor – to investigate the report's allegations".

There is also the problem for consumers of the proliferation of certification schemes. How do they understand which ones do what? Should they believe some more than others? Or do they do what most people do and simply take the brand itself on trust?

The only way to build trust is through greater transparency. All organisations have to get used to the fact that all stakeholders, internal and external, have an insatiable thirst for more information. Not all of them will look closely, but the fact that they can is reassurance enough.

Others may use the information to challenge the organisation and attempt to hold it to account. More transparency is one level, but organisations need to think beyond that. How can they be held to account? What mechanisms can be used and applied? Responding through social media is certainly one possibility.

Once transparency is applied to one part of an organisation, then it will be ratcheted up and applied to others as well. Once the shaft of light comes in, there is no stopping it.

But, as already noted, expectations change over time. What was acceptable once can be unacceptable in the future. That comes through very strongly in the concern for the environment, but also personal behaviour as well.

The focus on the environment will only get more acute. Even those organisations which are not necessarily exploiting the environment for production purposes will have to demonstrate how they are moving towards the new net zero targets.

Countries around the world have signed up to achieving net zero targets, but without having a plan about to get there. That means those who have signed up to the Paris Agreement have agree to deliver carbon neutrality by the second half of the 21st century.

But the UK has gone further, at least symbolically, and became the world's first major economy to pass a net zero emissions law. The law, passed in June 2019, means that all greenhouse gas emissions will need to be net zero by 2050.

Individual sectors are being pushed harder as well, especially the automotive sector. Norway has set a 2025 target for all new cars to be zero-emission models. The UK recently moved forward its commitment to banning the sale of new petrol, diesel and hybrid cars from 2040 to 2035.

Even those organisations which have set themselves some pretty challenging targets need to work out how best to deliver on their ambitions. That means all parts of an organisation's operation need to be seen through a zero emissions lens. Whilst governments may talk big, the delivery side is being given much less attention.

Then studies suggest that the use of the internet, streaming, emails etc. could be responsible for the same level of carbon emissions as the airlines industry. There is some dispute about the figures, but the overall message is that whatever sector you operate in, action against emissions is needed.

The challenge for businesses is that whilst governments may pass impressive-sounding laws about carbon reduction, they lack ideas about how to implement them. That presents both a reputational challenge and an opportunity.

Lesson – Your operational environment is constantly changing, and that brings reputational opportunities and threats

---

There is no doubt that governments will expect businesses to come up with solutions to the climate change challenge.

The European Investment Bank launched a new climate strategy at the end of 2019 in which it promised to end the financing of fossil fuel energy projects from the end of 2021 and "will align all financing activities with the goals of the Paris Agreement from the end of 2020".[21]

For organisations, that undoubtedly means considering all aspects of their operations and seeing where action can be taken. Energy usage is a base line, but they must also consider supply chain issues, how employees travel etc. It is all very well expecting workers to remote work more frequently, but what about the equipment they use and the energy they consume offsite? Just because an organisation "centrally" has reduced its consumption, that does not mean that its overall operations have.

As some organisations have found to their cost, simply having policies in place but failing to have the rigorous policing needed just leads to trouble. Codes, standards and ethical requirements need to be constantly checked and verified.

Lesson – All parts of an organisation's operation need to be seen through a zero emissions lens, and that focus will become more acute

---

Those organisations at the frontline of climate change – energy generation, travel etc. – need to deliver the solutions to government. If they fail to do so, then they, at the very least, face reputational risk through being "named and shamed", but more than that, they run the very real risk of ill-conceived direct regulatory and legislative intervention.

Anti-business sentiment is already high, and has been growing, as documented in the results of the Edelman Trust Barometer. If politicians then start blaming business for the failure to address climate change, which results in missing the targets set down in law, then the reputation implications increase still further. There are other consequences, too. The insurer Beazley believes that it is facing higher damages payouts because of anti-business sentiment in the US. The insurance sector blames "social inflation" for causing such higher financial costs as US juries suggest higher damages against businesses.

One of the ways in which organisations can show that they are taking their ESG responsibilities seriously is to partner with others who can help them along their journey.

I spoke to Pauliina Murphy, Engagement Director and co-founder of the World Benchmarking Alliance, about its work to try to generate a movement around increasing the private sector's impact towards a sustainable future for all.

Pauliina explained that the United Nations' Sustainable Development Goals (SDGs) were launched in 2015 and represented a hugely ambitious political agenda, aimed at making sustainable development a reality. The 17 SDGs cover all aspects of life, from ending poverty and hunger to providing water and sanitation for all, from reaching gender equality to ensuring sensible consumption within planetary boundaries. Achieving the goals will require large-scale and profound transformations of the ecological, industrial, technological, financial and human systems that generate or perpetuate economic, environmental and social pressures.

The reality is that the delivery of the SDGs will not be cheap, so it is not a responsibility for governments alone. Instead, it needs business, and finance in particular, to play a new role, collaborating more closely on joint projects and initiatives with governments and other actors, embedding the targets of the SDGs in core business practices, operations and value chains.

For Pauliina, "the SDGs are a roadmap for all stakeholders, not just the governments of developing countries". Until their launch, the private sector had little direct engagement with the UN, but given the size of the task and the acceptance of the role that the private sector has to play, companies have been slowly let into the heart of the multi-governmental system.

She believes that the fact that business leaders are now, on occasion, invited to join discussions on the financing agenda and provide advice could be one reason why there is greater general awareness of the SDGs. It was thanks to the UN Global Compact that the then Chief Executive Officer of the global insurance company Aviva, Mark Wilson, was given a speaking slot in the General Assembly Hall of the UN to present why companies like Aviva needed to take this agenda seriously. According to Wilson:

> I've always been crystal clear why I'm in business: to make a greater positive impact each year on the lives of our customers and clients and society as a whole. Making a profit is a by-product – albeit a very important one – of that core activity. In business, we create financial value for shareholders – but only if we create a wider social value for customers and society.

There are similarities here with some of the positions highlighted earlier in the chapter and point to a realisation that the very nature of business has changed, together with a realisation on the part of the government and others of that change.

There are also real economic opportunities to be gained by businesses if they engage with the SDGs. The Business and Sustainable Development Commission (BSDC) flagship report *Better Business, Better World* found that companies embracing the SDGs could unlock more than US$12 trillion in market opportunities and create up to 380 million new jobs by 2030 in just four sectors alone. This market incentive, combined with the increased demand from consumers for products and services that meet their changing needs as they make more value-based purchase decisions, has undoubtedly, according to Murphy, "made many companies stand up and take notice of the SDGs".

Pointing to the implications of COVID-19, Pauliina Murphy is firmly of the opinion that:

> the companies that continue to take care of their people through the COVID-19 crisis, be it in their operations or supply chains, will be rewarded and at the front and centre of the efforts to rebuild the

global economy. Their purpose and value-based actions during this time will emerge as an imperative for long-term success.

However, after five years, the world is not on track to achieve the UN's SDGs. But rather than slow, piecemeal change, Pauliina and her colleagues are looking for businesses to transform themselves "from inside out".

She indicates that there are many examples of benchmarks and indices which help investors make decisions based on ESG issues. Many are focused on financial materiality, so the financial impact of the sustainability risk on the company's balance sheet. What benchmarks enable investors and others to do is take an evidence-based approach to challenge poorly performing companies or recognise and incentivise those companies that do well.

Research has shown that workers' communities, investors, consumers and civil society are empowered with better information to negotiate with companies based on the information produced in reports. The benchmarks enable them to compare the companies and use that information to make well-informed decisions about how to engage and with which companies.

Often the information sits behind a paywall and is used by the large investment houses, but individual investors cannot access it. The establishment of the World Benchmarking Alliance (WBA) is designed to change this lack of available information. Its mission is to provide comparable information on company behaviour and give it away freely. The WBA will develop benchmarks to measure companies' progress against the SDGs.

This marks a move away from measuring sustainability risk to measuring the impact of companies on people and the planet. It is working on new sets of methodologies and indicators that consider impact in systems, measuring corporate policies and practices as well as supply chains – for example, the working conditions of female workers in garment factories in Bangladesh.

Data like these are still hard to come by, but by engaging directly with the private sector and other stakeholders in building the methodologies, the WBA believes that its transparent and comparable benchmarks will reveal both to companies and stakeholders where each company stands compared to its peers, where it can improve, and where urgent action is needed for it to deliver on the SDGs in its business strategies, operations, supply chains, and product and service portfolios. The benchmarks empower stakeholders, from consumers and investors to employees and business leaders, with key data and insights to encourage sustainable business practices across all sectors.

In terms of the benchmarks themselves, Pauliina believes that they "become credible when companies see that they translate the expectations of their key stakeholders (customers, employees, investors and others). Benchmark methodologies should therefore be based on scientific and societal expectations and their development needs to involve companies".

The companies can then use the benchmarks to help them target their activities as well as to identify where they are restricted by regulations, policies or other standards and norms. They may then want to engage with governments in trying to remove them. They can also help in internally bridging gaps in understanding and mindset such as between boards and front-line staff.

Once the benchmarks are published and presented as league tables, they can harness companies' competitive spirit and promote a "race to the top". By virtue of being public and due to the way in which the data are presented, these benchmarks empower all stakeholders, from consumers and investors to employees and business leaders.

They also keep organisations on a path as well. Once committed to delivering sustainability, it will be near impossible to change course. But to fall back in a league table will bring with it its own pressures, not least on reputation. It is all very well being number one, but what happens to a reputation if an organisation starts falling down the list?

But, as Pauliina went on to highlight:

> investor, employee and customer expectations of companies they want to invest in and do business with are changing daily and fundamentally. These stakeholders are starting to reward the businesses making courageous choices on sustainability. With the COVID-19 crisis, the long-term legacy we leave behind for those we

love seems to be more critical than ever. The closer we get to the SDG 2030 deadline, the more attention will go on celebrating those businesses that are taking real and meaningful action and on challenge those who are not, or businesses that don't "walk the talk".

As the WBA would see it, the right actions can have positive and long-standing consequences on societies and ecosystems and should be incentivised. It has identified a list of the world's 2,000 most influential keystone companies on the SDGs. These are the companies that the WBA will measure and rank across seven systems, be it on digital inclusion, food and agriculture or energy and decarbonisation. The WBA will assess both their negative and positive impacts and measure their contributions to achieving systemic change across the systems in which they operate. Keystone companies are those that are dominant globally, with power and influence across suppliers, governments and other networks.

Being on the list brings with it opportunities for those companies. They can, if they choose, demonstrate and communicate their commitment and leadership on the SDGs to their employees, customers and investors: "Companies that follow words with actions are likely to see big reputational gains; and companies that don't behave in a way that society expects them to, will be found out".

Pauliina detailed the example of the Seafood Stewardship Index launched in October 2019, which shows the impact that accountability and scrutiny can have on a company's reputation, but also the way in which this reputation can be rebuilt through a detailed understanding of the building blocks that need to be put in place on sustainability. The Index is the first of its kind, and ranks global seafood companies on their SDG impact. The Thai Union Group, one of the world's largest global seafood companies, tops the list of companies and now has in place strong sustainability strategies, sourcing and human rights policies, as evidenced by its number one position on the ranking. However, in 2015 it was at the centre of a scandal about widespread use of the most grotesque forms of modern-day slavery in the Thai seafood industry and beyond. At the time, Thai Union rightly faced huge criticism from media, retailers, governments and investors. The company has stepped up since, and while its journey to embed sustainable business practices is not yet over, it is now leading the industry in terms of traceability and eradicating the use of forced labour on fishing vessels.

The WBA recognises that consumers are making more value-based purchase decisions, employees prefer to work for sustainable brands and investors are reallocating capital in line with impact, which places a new emphasis on companies' responsibility and long-term reputation.

Research conducted by data and measurement-driven agency Essence in spring 2020 for its report *Advertising in 2030* notes that:

> The next 10 years belong to GenZ, who will drive culture, consumerism, and companies in that direction. Companies that don't adhere to environmental codes and even stricter ones in the years to come will simply vanish.

If a company is in the scope of a benchmark, it will be subject to regular measurement. Any gaps of inaction will be highlighted. Clear, accessible and comparable information will be available to inform investment and purchase decision-making. Companies are, in effect, on notice that they need to be purpose-led, ensure sustainability is embedded in their services and products, and recognise that profitability doesn't come at any cost.

Pauliina contends that:

> benchmarks are not rigid – they need to be updated on a regular basis to ensure that company progress is tracked alongside developments in regulation, policy, and standards and changing consumer expectations. They serve as roadmaps for companies on the steps they can take to take responsibility for their workers, stakeholders, society at large and the health of our planet.

Lesson – Consider the role of benchmarks: they help show a path to improvement and incentivise best practice, and this is will deliver improvements in reputation

---

Business-to-business

The moves towards sustainability by organisations can be seen as a central aspect not just of good operational practices, but of reputation management as well. There is not a single organisation that not does need to give consideration to their environmental impact.

Some may think very narrowly in terms of their own reputation. Others may be trying to ensure that they are not outmanoeuvred by competitors or may be being "forced" to think in a more environmental way by consumer demands. However, it should not be forgotten that corporates are consumers as well. Business-to-business (B2B) is a critical market as much as business-to-consumer (B2C) is. Much of the writing on reputation management tends to concentrate on the B2C side of the equation, but for many organisations their consumers are other businesses.

Many businesses will demand exacting standards of those they do business with. The ways in which they choose who works for them places requirements in the way. These could cover everything from the way small business payments are processed through to demands on labour standards and environmental achievements.

Why put such requirements in place? As we have seen from the examples across fast fashion, the behaviour of your suppliers reflects on you just as much as, say, the behaviour of your own directly employed staff.

If the requirements are clearly stipulated, then if they are broken, you can take action. And, thinking narrowly about reputation, it allows you to show publicly that rules exist and action has been taken – exactly what stakeholders will want to hear.

Carolina Gasparoli is the Head of Communications, at Cornerstone Barristers. As she told me, the Bar is "an old and well-established institution, with long-standing traditions that have a strong influence on the way its members perceive themselves and their relationship with the external world".

That has led to an "inherent suspicion towards self-promotion and self-advertising, certainly among the old guard, and it is only fairly recently that certain rules have been relaxed by lifting the ban on barristers' advertising, making it similar to solicitors'".

But this is starting to change, especially amongst a younger generation: "there is a perception that your personal brand as well as your chambers' brand is important in terms of attracting and retaining good work, and in terms of career development". It is also the case that, just as with other services, the public, or those buying services from barristers, "wants and expects to know more about what is available from different lawyers", so this makes marketing, legal communications and reputation central to the conversation.

For Carolina, the new relationship between the profession and social media, from a regulatory point of view as well as a reputational one, is worth considering in more detail. She highlights that the media has reported a few cases of disciplinary action against members of the barrister profession for posting offensive comments on social media, a behaviour that has been found likely to diminish the trust and confidence of the public:

> Members of the Bar are self-employed, and there is often a temptation of thinking of themselves as acting in their personal capacity. In my view, there is an unresolved tension within the profession between the "individual", represented by the individual barrister, and the "collective", the chambers they belong to and, more widely, the profession as a whole.

This may be a very pronounced situation that barristers face, but it could be argued that the same fundamental challenge faces leaders. They have their own reputations, but are they ever really detached from the organisations that employ them? I would suggest not.

Carolina suggests:

> Many barristers would argue that there is a clear division between themselves in their role as members of the profession and their belonging to a Chambers, and their private life. Things are not that simple and the division is not as straightforward as they argue. In October 2019, the Bar Standards Board [BSB] issued new guidance warning that barristers would face disciplinary action for inappropriate use of social media even if they believe they are doing so in their private capacity.

Carolina recognises that the barrister profession is often perceived as having a "PR problem", particularly in relation to social media. She points to the tone and content of social media posts:

There are hundreds of "PR" incidents on social media that, even if they don't have disciplinary consequences, show poor judgement for getting involved in such debates in the first place. Often, the desire to help explain the law, a legal or policy decision, or simply to express a personal point of view, has disastrous consequences from a reputational point of view.

Some members of the profession have already expressed their frustration at their colleagues for being pompous, sanctimonious or pedantic. The fact that barristers are first and foremost advocates, often leads them think that every forum is the same. It's not. Being in court is not the same as being on Twitter and the tone - and content – one should deploy is not the same. Advocacy is not the same as communications and the skills required, although with some overlapping, are not identical.

Then comes the reputational damage on themselves and their Chambers. The wider ramifications caused by their online presence requires "a deeper awareness of the reputational damage at stake for the individual as well as for their Chambers".

As with other leaders, there is a danger that the position one reaches brings with it a self-confidence that prevents wider self-awareness. In simplistic terms, instead of taking advice, they believe that they can do it. That could be applied to social media, political engagement, media statements or a wide range of other potentially reputation-damaging situations.

Carolina suggests a number of potential remedies:

- Have a social media policy that is up to date with recent regulation.
- Have social media training.
- Be open to discuss "dos" and "don'ts" when it comes to external communications.
- Involve communications specialists who can help you understand how to manage your personal reputation.
- Don't forget traditional media. Stay close to journalists and opinion makers in your field as much as your obligations towards the court and the clients allow you to, so you can be in control of the message.

Future needs?

As supply chains have become global, we have seen more questions being asked not just about the environmental credentials, but increasingly their human rights records as well. Catie Shavin, Director of the Global Business Initiative on Human Rights, believes that:

> In recent years, we've seen a significant shift in how seriously businesses and other organisations are taking human rights issues and challenges. Ten years ago, few companies were comfortable talking about human rights issues or expressing human rights commitments. Now, human rights policies and due diligence processes are becoming increasingly commonplace – at least among the largest and most brand-exposed multinational businesses.
>
> Authoritative global standards – the UN Guiding Principles on Business and Human Rights (UNGPs) – were adopted in 2011. These standards set out the respective roles of business and governments in addressing business-related human rights challenges and provided a practical roadmap for organisations to follow. By clarifying who should do what, the UNGPs have helped transform talk into action.

There is, though, she believes:

> a long way to go to realise the vision of all companies, everywhere, operating with respect for human rights. The challenges of achieving this vision should not be understated. Many business and human rights challenges, such as modern slavery, are both complex and systemic, and require significant co-operation from diverse stakeholders around the world to address. And more is needed to build effective incentives for smaller and less brand-exposed companies around the world to take their human rights risk management seriously. That said, the growing momentum and commitment behind companies' efforts to address business and human rights issues is encouraging.

Catie fully believes that the emerging trend towards companies and other organisations taking their human rights risk management seriously will increase. She points to a number of developments driving this:

- A transformation catalysed by COVID-19: the suggestions by governments that we "build back better" place a spotlight on systemic and structural challenges associated with social and economic systems.
- Climate change and just transitions: the significant transitions our societies and economies will go through in the coming years and decades as a result of climate change pose significant risks to people. So it is crucial that respect for human rights is "baked into" climate change decision-making processes, to support just transitions and minimise harms to people.
- The changing legal landscape: the business and human rights legal landscape is changing, and expectations of business are beginning to harden. While the UNGPs are not voluntary – failure to meet the expectations they set out can result in very real risks to business – they are not legally binding. However, these expectations are increasingly reflected in domestic legal requirements.

For companies, and others, the challenge is how they can build respecting human rights into all aspects of their operations. As with other aspects of reputation management, organisations need to show that they are managing the risks associated with human rights. Shavin suggests that this can be done by:

- Making a clear commitment to meeting their human rights responsibilities and embedding that in the organisation's "rights-respecting culture".
- Implement an ongoing human rights due diligence process "that enables the organisation to know what its human rights impacts are and to take effective steps to address those". That would include their own risks as well as those associated with those they do business with. "The key difference between human rights due diligence and other types of due diligence is that human rights due diligence should focus on identifying risks to people, rather than risks to the business, and be informed by meaningful engagement with stakeholders".
- Participating in or providing access to remedies where they cause or contribute to a negative impact.

As is the case with other aspects of risks, a number of benchmarks have been established, such as Corporate Human Rights and Know the Chain. These benchmarks make it easier for stakeholders, including investors, to make comparisons between what companies say and do, but also between companies. All this brings extra pressure on reputations.

Human rights, it seems, will be of growing importance in reputation terms. As more organisations fail to take a clear and effective line, the more the impact of human rights will be appreciated. However, Catie Shavin believes that much more needs to be done:

> I still see too many organisations taking a superficial approach to respecting human rights. They communicate well about their human rights commitments and processes, but are not sufficiently backing this up with effective human rights due diligence. Effective action to identify and address human rights risks is critical to enable meaningful positive outcomes for affected people and to manage the reputational risks. When things go wrong, being able to demonstrate that public commitments were supported by robust efforts to manage human rights issues is key to maintaining and re-building trust with stakeholders.
>
> As new regulatory requirements drive global brands to ensure robust human rights risk management across their value chains, it will become more important that their suppliers and other business partners be able to demonstrate that they can meet expectations.

The activist agenda

Employee activism is on the rise. More organisations are having to respond as much to what their employees think about their operations as other, outside, stakeholders.

These employees are another way in which organisations are being held to account for their actions and behaviours. They are happy to do so in a very public way and "name and shame" their own organisation.

Often the numbers involved are not huge, but the very fact that a group of like-minded employees feels so strongly as to come together and put a spotlight on behaviour can be a powerful driver of change. In many ways, these activist employees know that they are hurting the reputation of the organisation they work for, and that, in itself, can secure change. Such reputational damage, inflicted by the very people who have most to lose, always resonates more. They are certainly listened to by others, not least the media. In some ways, it is the ultimate method of inflicting reputational damage. What could be worse than your own people suggesting that you are acting in a wrong – or worse, hypocritical – way?

Weber Shandwick's *Employee Activism in the Age of Purpose*,[22] a survey of 1,000 employed Americans adults, found that:

- 71% of employees feel they can make a difference in society, with 62% believing they can make a greater impact than business leaders can. Millennials are significantly more likely than older generations to feel empowered.
- Most US employees believe employees are right to speak up about their employers, whether they are in support of them (84%) or against (75%).
- 38% of American employees have spoken up to support or criticize their employer's actions over a controversial issue that affects society. Millennials are significantly more likely to be Employee Activists than older generations (48% versus 33% of Gen Xers and 27% of Boomers).
- While 38% of employees are Employee Activists, an additional 11% are Potential Employee Activists, as they've considered speaking out. Millennials are most likely to be Employee Activists or potential Employee Activists (61%), followed by Gen Xers (44%) and Boomers (37%).

In some countries, there are trade unions, workplace boards and other formal mechanisms to channel such "activism", but that does guarantee that issues will not be aired in public. The figures here, whilst US-based, appear to be more widely applicable. We see a younger generation more willing to speak out and use the power of an organisation's reputation against it to try to secure change.

Lesson – Activists can be inside as much as outside your organisation

Quoted in the *Seattle Times*, Sujatha Bergen, Director of Health Campaigns at the Natural Resources Defense Council, said:

> Young people – millennials, Generation Z and whoever else comes after that – they are worried about climate change. Those are the customers that a company like Starbucks wants to capture, and if they are seen [by Wall Street] as out of touch with that customer base, then that is a major risk.[23]

Just as organisations want to try to appeal to these groups as consumers, they also need to think about how to work with them as employees.

As with all forms of communication and engagement, the essential steps are to manage the risk and then have a plan to deal with it. If the issue can be dealt with before employees feel the need to go public, then the risk has been managed effectively.

The heart of employee activism is often showing up the difference between organisational commitment and delivery.

Commitment versus delivery

Organisations will often make grand claims about their actions, but as mentioned right at the start of the book, a gap can exist between the reality and the rhetoric. To the outside world, that is not always obvious. To those on the inside, who have sight of information and behaviours, the gap is more obvious.

Greenpeace has been calling on Amazon, Google and Microsoft to reinforce their commitments to tackling climate change by ending the sale of their technologies to the oil and gas sector. The group made its call following the announcement by founder and CEO of Amazon Jeff Bezos to invest $10 billion of his own money into projects designed to tackle climate change. The Bezos Earth Fund was announcement by Bezos himself on Instagram.

But Amazon employees had already come together the banner of Amazon Employees for Climate Justice (AECJ) to champion the company itself taking action to ensure that it doesn't contribute to climate change or environmental racism.

Hundreds of employees also used the hashtag #AMZNSpeakOut to condemn the company for not doing enough to tackle climate change.

The list of examples of companies facing internal revolts keeps getting longer:

- Google – a post on Medium and a petition against any support for US government agencies engaging in "human rights abuses". This was launched at a time when Google was making a decision about whether to bid for a government cloud computing contract.
- Wayfair – employees staged a walkout from its headquarters in Boston to protest against the sale of furniture to child migrant detention facilities. The company subsequently donated $100,000 to the Red Cross, but this too came in for criticism.
- Hachette Book Group – it decided not to publish a memoir by Woody Allen, the director, actor and writer, who has been accused of sexual abuse, after its employees walked out.
- Microsoft – it has encountered a number of employee reactions against the company's position. Dozens of employees signed a letter protesting the company's $480 million contract to supply the US Army with augmented-reality headsets intended for use on the battlefield. Also, an open letter was posted to Microsoft's internal message board, signed by more than 100 employees, to protest against its work with US Immigration and Customs Enforcement. A critical statement from the letter was: "We are part of a growing movement, comprised of many across the industry who recognize the grave responsibility that those creating powerful technology have to ensure what they build is used for good, and not for harm".[24] Microsoft has also faced "in person" protests.
- Facebook – hundreds of employees signed a letter protesting at the company's decision to allow politicians to post false statements in advertisements on the social media site. After some delay, Twitter took action against comments made by President Trump by flagging them as being in violation of the company's policies. However, Facebook did not, so its employees reacted by posting public comments, staging a virtual walkout, and several resigned and others threatened to. According to reports, a Q&A session addressed

by Zuckerberg and watched by 25,000 employees was particularly fraught.

What can be seen is that these are not random demands, but instead focus on attempts to hold the companies to the standards that they themselves have set. It could be suggested that it is another way that the companies are being held to account.

Organisations need to factor in employee participation in the development of policies and strategies, but can also expect them to have a continuing voice.

If they feel that are being bound into a process but then effectively silenced, either because of a deficient internal procedure or because the corporate position prevents them from speaking out, then they will find other ways to make their voices heard. For example, internal documents often find their way into the hands of leading publications or are posted online.

This forces the companies to take a public position. An organisation needs to be able and prepared to defend itself and stand up for its decisions. This needs to be considered from the outset. If it is not possible to defend it, then go back and question the initial decision.

Lesson – *Activists hold you to account, often in a very public way*

Not just employees ...

A key aspect of reputation management is also understanding more about the motivations and tactics of campaigning organisations. Companies, charities, higher education institutions – none are immune from being campaigned against. It is not just large campaigning organisations either. Very small groups can be highly effective and can grow and build support over time. Never underestimate a campaign. Always take their position and aims seriously. Action at the outset could be the most effective way of dealing with a campaign. It could easily stop it becoming bigger and more powerful over time.

> *Lesson – Activists will often understand your organisational rulebook better than you do*

That is not to say that organisations should simply give in to make a problem go away. But if the campaign is considered and no change is required then, the time should still be taken to respond. It may not placate the campaign, but it will mean that steps taken can be explained and demonstrates a constructive approach to engagement. That can only be good in protecting a reputation.

Campaigns can take many forms, but the most effective ones are:

1) Focus on behaviour.
2) Demonstrate gaps between reality and rhetoric.
3) Build support – people, finance, online, the media, politics.
4) Target an organisation where it will hurt it most, such as sales.
5) Set out a clear agenda for change.

Campaigns will also consider the legal options open to them. "Shareholder activism" is now part of everyday corporate life, and resolutions at AGMs have become a favourite opportunity for activists to exert pressure. Few are instantly effective, but they are happy to shine a spotlight on action and apply the pressure over a period of time.

The example mentioned previously, the AECJ, worked with the Center for Community Action on Environmental Justice (CCAEJ) to file a resolution at Amazon's AGM asking the board to address environmental racism.

The resolution read:

> Shareholders request that Amazon prepare a public report, describing its efforts, above and beyond legal and regulatory compliance, to identify and reduce disproportionate environmental and health harms to communities of color, associated with past, present and future pollution from its delivery logistics and other operations. The report should be prepared at reasonable expense and may exclude confidential information.

This is another example of not just doing what is legally required, but going beyond that. The legal requirement, again, should be considered as the base level.

Sometimes these resolutions are clever ways for small groups to raise an issue. They may buy the minimum number of shares needed to table a resolution which secures them the attention they need. On other occasions, the resolutions are tabled by bigger, more institutional shareholders also seeking change.

The Dutch group "Follow This", which focuses on climate change, has been targeting ExxonMobil, Chevron, Royal Dutch Shell, BP and Equinor by buying minor stakes in the companies and using that as a completely legal opportunity to file a resolution.

> *Lesson – Activists will use all the tools available to them and will not be afraid to disrupt operations*

Wrong decisions

Even the most cursory of examinations of crises reveal that they are very often self-inflicted.

Organisations often get it right and read the tone of public opinion in making swift decisions. Take the example of Steve Easterbrook, the CEO of McDonald's. When he was found to have had a consensual relationship with an employee against company rules, he was immediately removed. There was no fudging the position, and the company rules were clear. Easterbrook himself, in an email to employees reported in the media, said: "This was a mistake …. Given the values of the company, I agree with the board that it is time for me to move on".

The company looked like it has taken swift action, in line with societal expectations. McDonald's has long faced allegations of sexual harassment, and the new CEO made it plain that he was looking to change the corporate culture of the organisation. The opportunity for potentially significant change was opened up by what was essentially a well-handled crisis.

Even the initial statement from the company focused on "leadership transition" and the new CEO. It was all very positive and forward-looking. Chris Kempczinski had been named President and CEO, with Easterbrook having "separated". Following a large picture of Kempczinski, there was one line on why Easterbrook had left. Nothing was hidden, but it was not the major part of the story, as McDonald's saw it. Then there was another separate release on Kempczinski's replacement as head of the US division. So again, business as usual – a bright future and forcing the less pleasant news further down the website page.

Since that initial golden phase, allegations of sexual misconduct have come to light about Easterbrook and, at the time of writing, he is being sued by the company. McDonald's has also been showing its support for Black Lives Matter on Twitter, through an advertising campaign and a very significant contribution to the National Association for the Advancement of Colored People, but against a backdrop of black former franchisees and former executives suing them for racial discrimination. Kempczinski's comment that "probably, McDonald's has created more millionaires within the Black community than probably any other corporation on the planet, but there's still work to do" was not universally well received.

Lesson – Dealing with the reputational fallout from one crisis is no guarantee of future success, so maintain a constant watch

---

On occasions, organisations can bring on a crisis all by themselves – often by trying to execute what might, on the face of it, be a sensible shift. In the case of Gillette, in trying to give its "the best a man can get" slogan a #MeToo makeover and address the problem of toxic masculinity, it simply invoked a backlash. "The best a man can be" joined a long list of adverts that did little to improve reputations, such as:

- Pepsi – Kendall Jenner deescalates a protest with the aid of a can.
- Nivea – the "White is Purity" campaign.
- Dove – black models becoming white after using a product.

- Protein World – beach body-ready.
- Peloton – Christmas ad where a woman is given a bike by her partner.

A good example of a calculated risk approach was designed to get the fast-food chain KFC out of a crisis of its own making. Following a change in its delivery arrangements in the UK, the chain ran out of chicken and had to close hundreds of outlets. The reaction was a mix of outrage and comedy, but there was the more serious element of a chicken outlet that couldn't supply chicken. That is pretty central to whole concept of KFC.

Once the delivery issue had been sorted, the company decided to try to be a little cheeky with its own brand to grab the agenda back again. It took out full-page adverts in the *Sun* and *Metro* newspapers with an image of an empty KFC bucket with a few crumbs around it. Underneath the image was a full apology, starting with "We're sorry". But instead of carrying the new logo, the letters on the bucket had been switched about to say "FCK".

It takes a very brave organisation to play with its own brand, but it meant that the apology is remembered as much as the initial disaster.

Attack culture

All organisations should be prepared for an attack. That is not to encourage a siege mentality or paranoia, but an appreciation that it forms part of good risk management.

The attacks can come from individuals as much as organised campaign groups, and they can grow in importance over time. All complaints, inquiries, Freedom of Information requests etc. should be taken seriously and responded to in a way that reflects the importance of reputation.

It is not a case of throwing time, effort and resources at the smallest enquiry, but instead having a process in place that escalates them if, for instance, a number come in on the same issue.

I would recommend that communications teams have an opportunity to look and consider, if only in the outline of the approach, all external communications. It is all too easy to respond in a technical manner or with too much jargon. Sometimes it is as much about connecting the dots as it is a technically correct response.

A failure to connect the dots – issues or people – can lead to a reputational challenge, one that could easily have been averted. These are always the worst type of situations to face because you could have done more to avoid them.

Notes

1 I consider this in Thomson (2020).
2 Armstrong and Narwan (2020).
3 Armstrong and Griffiths (2020).
4 See O'Connor (2018).
5 Thomson and John (2003).
6 FTI Consulting (2020).
7 Ibid.
8 Clayton (2019) (https://hbr.org/2019/12/6-signs-your-corporate-culture-is-a-liability).
9 BlackRock (n.d.) (www.blackrock.com/uk/intermediaries/about-us/about-blackrock).
10 Fink (2022) (www.blackrock.com/corporate/investor-relations/larry-fink-ceo -letter).
11 Warnick (2020) (https://stories.starbucks.com/emea/stories/2020/5-things-to -know-about-starbucks-new-environmental-sustainability-commitment/).
12 Motion Picture Association (2019) (www.motionpictures.org/press/major-film- and-television-studios-expand-sustainability-efforts-donate-over-130000 -meals-in-2018/).
13 Stewart (2020).
14 Hume (2019).
15 LME (2019) (www.lme.com/en-GB/About/Responsibility/Responsible-sourcing).
16 BBC (2020) (www.bbc.co.uk/news/technology-51518773).
17 Knowles (2020) (www.thetimes.co.uk/article/facebook-founder-mark-zucker- berg-agrees-that-he-may-have-to-pay-more-tax-35sjsz8mb).
18 PEFC (2014) (www.pefc.org/news/consumers-trust-certification-labels-and-exp ect-companies-to-label-products-pefc-research-shows).
19 Siddique (2019) (www.theguardian.com/business/2019/dec/22/tesco-halts-pro- duction-at-chinese-factory-over-forced-labour-claims-christmas-cards).
20 Ibid.
21 European Investment Bank (2019) (www.eib.org/en/press/all/2019-313-eu-bank -launches-ambitious-new-climate-strategy-and-energy-lending-policy).
22 Weber Shandwick (2019).
23 Roberts (2020).
24 Frenkel (2018).

Reference list

Ashley Armstrong and Gurpreet Narwan, 'Review of sweatshops no relief as Boohoo shares tumble again', *The Times*, 9 July 2020.
Ashley Armstrong and Katherine Griffiths, 'Aberdeen standard investments dumps Boohoo shares over pay scandal', *The Times*, 10 July 2020.

BBC, 'Mark Zuckerberg: Facebook boss urges tighter regulation', 15 February 2020, https://www.bbc.co.uk/news/technology-51518773.

BlackRock, 'Actually it's never been about us', https://www.blackrock.com/uk/intermediaries/about-us/about-blackrock, n.d.

Business and Sustainable Development Commission, 'Better business, better world', January 2016.

Edelman Trust Barometer. https://www.edelman.com/trust/archive

European Investment Bank, 'EU Bank launches ambitious new climate strategy and energy lending policy', 14 November 2019.

FTI Consulting, 'Resilience barometer 2020: Build resilience, protect value', January 2020.

Haroon Siddique, 'Tesco withdraws Christmas cards from sale after forced labour claims', *The Guardian*, 22 December 2019.

Ipsos, 'Unlocking the value of reputation: The definitive link between corporate reputation and better business efficiency', May 2018.

Jennifer Warnick, '5 things to know about Starbucks new environmental sustainability commitment', *Starbucks Stories & News*, 21 January 2020.

Kate Scott-Dawkins and Mark Syal, 'Advertising in 2030: Expert predictions on the future of advertising', 27 April 2020.

Larry Fink, 'Larry Fink's 2022 letter to CEOs: The power of capitalism', BlackRock, January 2022.

LME, *Responsible Sourcing*, October 2019.

Motion Picture Association, *Major Film and Television Studios Expand Sustainability Efforts; Donate Over 130,000 Meals in 2018*, 22 April 2019.

Neil Hume, 'LME to shake up rules on responsibly sourced metals', *Financial Times*, 23 April 2019.

Paul Roberts, 'Starbucks' sustainability plan sets 'Resource Positive' Goal', *The Seattle Times*, 22 January 2020.

PEFC, 'Consumers trust certification labels and expect companies to label products, PEFC research shows', 20 November 2014.

Rebecca Stewart, 'Is climate change denial a brand safety issue?', *The Drum*, 19 February 2020.

Sarah Clayton, '6 signs your corporate culture is a liability', *Harvard Business Review*, 5 December 2019.

Sarah O'Connor, 'Dark factories: Labour exploitation in Britain's garment industry', *Financial Times*, 17 May 2018.

Sheera Frenkel, ''Microsoft employees protest work with ICE', as tech industry mobilizes over immigration', *New York Times*, 19 January 2018 (including letter https://int.nyt.com/data/documenthelper/46 -microsoft-employee-letter-ice/323507fcbddb9d0c59ff/optimized/full .pdf#page=1).

Stuart Thomson, 'Why proactivity is the key to managing a reputation', *Signal AI White Paper*, July 2020.

Stuart Thomson and Steve John, *New Activism and the Corporate Response*, Palgrave, 2003.

Tom Knowles, 'Facebook founder Mark Zuckerberg agrees that he 'may have to pay more tax'', *The Times*, 14 February 2020.

Weber Shandwick, 'Employee activism in the age of purpose: Employees (up)rising', 29 May 2019.

3

THE MEDIA
A STUDY IN PRESSURE

The focus on the role of the media in reputation management tends to be highlighted when it comes to dealing with a crisis, but its role is so much wider than that. Along with social media, it plays a fundamental role in getting messages to stakeholder audiences but also motivating and engaging them.

The media, in all its forms, is not just about a crisis. It should be for everyday operations.

In this chapter, we explore ways in which organisations need to consider the media when managing reputation.

The fundamentals

The media used to be the be-all and end-all of communications. If you could work with the media, then you could go a fair way to protecting your reputation. But the position is now more complex. For one, the

DOI: 10.4324/9781003293880-4

media is no longer a monolith. It is more diffuse and diverse. That means the points where your weaknesses can be exposed are numerous. Plus, largely thanks to social media, power increasingly lies in the hands of individuals, not just large media conglomerates.

Nowadays, though, the media also needs to worry about its own reputation. The BBC is an institution that was founded in 1922. The media landscape has obviously changed hugely, but this has accelerated in recent years. The BBC remains known the world over, and the quality of its programming and journalism carry weight. That has not, however, meant that it is immune from criticism, especially at election time. It has come under attack from both the left and the right for allegedly showing bias. Many in the current Conservative government have been critical of the BBC and want to see significant reform. Reform appears to be coming, and a more US-style, privatised and subscription-based model is preferred by many.

Because the media itself is changing, that means that reputation management has had to change and develop as well.

The crisis

There can be a tendency to treat all bad stories as reputation-threatening and to over-react. Whilst it is always important to make a statement to get your side of the story across, an over-reaction will make matters worse.

Such over-reactions could typically include:

- Too much information in a statement – the detail will not be used, and your main points will be diluted.
- Keeping the story going over a longer period of time – keeping it alive by feeding it by providing more information.
- Feeling the need to go "nuclear" even at the most cursory of stories, maybe launching an inquiry or promising action against individuals when there is not the level of information to justify it.

Such an over-reaction would be loved by the media. It gives a much better story, and for any journalists concerned it will show how sensitive you are about the issue. Could that mean there is more to tell? If they dig further, will the "real story" come out?

This demonstrates how important it is for communications teams to consider the implications of their responses. Sometimes there is a need to take a few knocks.

As Alastair Campbell, the former communications director for Labour Prime Minister Tony Blair, has said: "You have to take ownership of your own strategic space".[1]

Any leader needs a team that helps to protect them and gets a grip of that strategic space. This is not the same as leaders being isolated. Instead, the team should take some of the hits and only bring issues to the leader that really require the leader's attention. A leader should not be the one ploughing through the tweets, reading the comments on a blog post or picking up the phone to the media.

Lawyers should be part of that team as well. They often get a bad press when it comes to dealing with a crisis, and are accused of lacking empathy or refusing to allow apologies to be given. Lawyers too often get blamed when the response to a crisis does not go according to plan.

But that is to misunderstand both the role of lawyers and what the role of communicators should be. Working effectively with lawyers in a team is about taking the time to understand them and their motivations. Many communicators, sadly, do not give this sufficient consideration.

The problem lies with communicators, not lawyers. Too often, communicators have not been able to come up with an appropriate form of words in response to a crisis, have not explained why the response is critical to the organisation or have not bothered to learn about the drivers of the legal advice.

Communicators can get too focused on the external communications – the statement – whilst neglecting what should be the other parts of their role. This includes building relationships with colleagues internally in advance of a crisis.

Good lawyers understand the value of communications and reputation, but many want to know that they are not going out on a limb. They like to learn from the experience and example of others. Precedent is incredibly important to them, so it could be that the answer to an "apology" issue is to show them what others have done and what has worked.

Communicators also have to appreciate what lawyers are there for. They offer protection. They protect the organisation from future liabilities and think about regulatory impacts and requirements. There may be certain things that from a communications perspective appear perfectly sensible, but legally you cannot say or do. Communicators should think about the pressures on the legal teams and help them to understand the communications concerns and timescales involved.

> Lesson – Build a good team who engage with one another in advance of a crisis

Too often, organisations believe that they understand everything about how the media works. But the best approach is not to expect balance or context. This places the onus on you to work afresh every time to consider how best to protect your reputation. It prevents lazy thinking.

A level of appreciation of what makes a good story means you are more able to assess the reputational challenges you face. A good network of media contacts can help educate you about what makes a media story. You must learn from them.

Whilst the emphasis is often placed on statements and messages when dealing with the media, it is always worth thinking about the role of visuals as well.

In a negative context, if there is imagery available that helps the media tell the story, then it helps make it a story. If you consider the distressing images that come with a natural or human-made disasters, you can understand why they feature so prominently across all media.

One reason why VW may not have suffered in the public image quite so much as other companies could be down to the inability to convey visually a faked emissions test in a laboratory.

The online game

Online now plays a critical role in the reputation of organisations and individuals.

Consider the ways in which people try to create their own reputations – LinkedIn profiles, fantastic and exotic images, and lives lived through Instagram and Facebook. But such actions are not simply a consequence of the online world. What better creates a reputation than an overplayed CV? This happened long before social media. But the ease with which impressions can be created is now of a different magnitude. These are all ways in which a person, or an organisation, can try to create a reputation. And people listen.

Authentic Communication in a Mistrusting World by Kantar[2] came up with a range of findings, all of which point to the critical nature of an online presence:

- 44% said their opinions of brands are influenced by what they read about them in online articles.
- 39% admitted they were influenced by the online comments and reviews of others.
- 50% of consumers said they trusted brand information found on the internet.
- 36% of consumers believed news, articles and features in print were good ways for brands to combat negative publicity.
- 28% of consumers believed news, articles and features online were good ways for brands to combat negative publicity.
- 47% saw TV and video as the best way to reach them.

There is a clear mix between the online world and the offline world. A reputation does not exist in one sphere in isolation from the other.

When it comes to getting brand information, the same report points to the following sources:

1) Internet and websites – 72%.
2) Friends and family – 53%.
3) Review sites – 44%.

So again, there is a mix of online and offline. It is important that organisations do not lose sight of the importance of their own websites and the online presence they control. Everything starts with what you say about yourself.

If you use that opportunity to bring a range of relevant information together in one place, then you can start to exert a greater level of control over conversations. Even journalists start their research by getting background information from your own site.

As with other communications channels, always think about the needs of the audiences. An online presence is not just for the media or consumers; policy-makers and politicians all refer online as a first step as well.

There are also issues to consider around the type of content that you want to feature online and how, for instance, to contend with search engine optimisation (SEO). This may mean featuring keywords that you want the search engines to pick up so that your presence ranks highly in their listing. This is only one aspect of SEO, which includes making content shareable and securing links to pages as well. In terms of reputation, it is clear that having your content ranked highly may provide welcome exposure over and above competitors. SEO is an important part of the online game.

There is a range of guides available about how to work best with Twitter, Instagram etc., but for professional audiences, LinkedIn is being increasingly used as a way of sharing and exchanging information.

Highlighting some of the best campaigns on LinkedIn in Canada, Jennifer Urbanski, its Senior Government Lead,[3] suggested a number of actions that had worked for the public sector, including sponsored content within the LinkedIn newsfeed. She also suggested that the activity of Canadian Prime Minister Justin Trudeau offered lessons to other users.[4]

Amongst the lessons were:

- Post often – to ensure that you stay "top-of-mind" with your network and to work through posts, comments, questions, likes and shares to maintain a variety of contact.
- Tag people or companies you mention – it increases the chances of engagement.
- Use hashtags – to help make content discoverable.

- Take the time to find strong images – posts with strong images perform better.
- Use LinkedIn's native video feature – it helps audiences to see who you really are.
- Be authentic – again, posts with authentic and personal content perform better.
- Engage with other people's content – to help develop the conversation and grow a professional brand.
- Add all your business contacts – it allows wider sharing of content and ideas.
- Follow other thought leaders – to enable you to learn from them as well.

If it is good enough for PM Trudeau, then there is something in this advice for all organisations!

Social media works best when it can turn the volume up on an issue. However, when leaders demand content that will "go viral", they appear to have two aspects in mind. One is related to a perception of low cost, the other is related to the speed and size of its impact and spread. That seems to them like the perfect way to amplify the name of an organisation.

But the chances of that happening are slim to zero. It is difficult, if not impossible, to predict. Viral content is usually thought about in a positive way, but the opposite is also true. Examples of poor behaviour can equally create viral content as well, causing its own reputational impacts.

Even the most cursory glance online will result in your finding examples of the staff at fast food companies failing to follow basic hygiene, delivery staff kicking packages around, violence by and against staff – the list is endless.

It is often genuine, user-generated content that provides the most telling contributions. During the early days of the COVID-19 outbreak, a heartfelt plea was made by a nurse in the UK, Dawn Bilbrough, for people to stop panic buying in supermarkets as it left her unable to buy basic items after completing a 48-hour shift.[5] The video was featured across the media and spurred the supermarkets into taking action, offering National Health Service (NHS) staff special hours.

From that came more of a focus on key workers, and a series of initiatives from government. For politicians, there is arguably nothing more damaging than a genuine comment from a member of the public that really seems to hit home. Politicians, like organisations, can choose to react in a number of ways. Those who can benefit from a comment that appears damaging are the ones who try to use it in a positive way. That means being prepared to listen and then respond with real and genuine actions. In the case of the nurse's video, the UK government and the supermarkets could see that she was speaking on behalf of all those working in the NHS and had identified a genuine problem. The Iceland supermarket chain had already offered a special hour for elderly, more vulnerable, shoppers. When the nurse's video went viral, a host of supermarkets moved quickly to offer NHS staff a similar concession.

Nurses, doctors, teachers and other key workers across the US, UK, Italy and even in China[6] used social media and direct appeals to make their concerns known. Each understood that they had a direct channel which could pick up views and bring welcome attention to their issues.

Listening does not always mean agreeing or "giving in" to demands, but if such viral content shows a weakness that should be addressed, then it provides the perfect opportunity to make it happen.

> *Lesson – Be prepared to respond with real action when called out, and use it as a positive opportunity*

An organisation can dig in and defend its behaviour or action, but always start by thinking through the consequences and the potential implications. Ask yourself whether it is the right thing to do. Also consider whether that defence can be continued over time. It may seem straightforward to respond in that way on day one or two, but could the same be said if more examples come out or the story continues over a period of weeks? Would you still continue on the same course of action, or would you then do something to address it? If that is the case, then get it over with on day one. Do not draw out the pain over an extended period of time only to then do something about it.

There are financial and personal costs of not taking immediate action, but also reputational impacts – not least being seen as an ineffective leader, as not really being in control or having been forced to take difficult decisions only after continued media or political pressure. That has personal career implications as well.

There are plenty of very good guides available about the use of social media, but from the outset leaders need to be aware that the "rules" of social media can be deeply uncomfortable and challenging:

1) You give up a large degree of control.
2) There needs to be clarity and consistency across channels.
3) Each social media channel is different, so there is no one way to behave.
4) Speed of response is important, but so is clarity and commitment.
5) Websites may seem old-fashioned nowadays, but they are still where many stakeholders, not least journalists and politicians, look for basic information.

Online personality

For leaders, social media offers the opportunity to share their personality and convey the ethics of the organisation they lead.

Bene't Steinberg, a public affairs stalwart in practice for 40 years, was keen to highlight the importance of the core values for any organisation when I spoke to him:

> Whatever media, marketing or Public Affairs strategy an organisation adopts, it must be in line with its core values, however these are expressed. Put simply, what you say and what you do must be congruent; one cannot tell the media one is a cuddly, likeable company whilst either ignoring customers or treating staff badly or wrecking the world. These blindingly simple statements are, strangely enough, often overlooked by organisations. They tend to be those who seek to tell the story they want known using straightforward "push" communications. Social media magnifies perceived differences between saying and doing far beyond the capacity of traditional media.

For Bene't:

> the best way to build reputation is to tell a version of how the organisation would like to be perceived that is aligned with (a) whatever metrics it has on how staff, customers and stakeholders perceive it, and (b) its branding propositions. In this, Social is the same as traditional communications. But Social can simultaneously magnify and diminish the stories. Done well, the impact of Social on highly targeted audiences can be massive. However, the sheer deluge of online chatter means that, if done without much thought, your message can simply drown. The principal challenge of Social is that your stories are best told in nutshell form: the Annual Report reduced to five one-liners, the brand proposition to a picture and four words. And each communication is subject to instant reaction from recipients – comments, likes, dislikes and, if you get it wrong, the dreaded Twitter-storm.
>
> He also believes strongly that an organisation *must* have a Social Media Manager, as:too many operations "look in occasionally" or "from time to time". That way lies the prospect of an ambush you could have seen coming, to hearing from random staff what's happening online, to being caught out of position if something kicks off. In short, Social takes resource and proper management time – it is not a toy or an add-on.

His plea, though, is not to get "seduced by the 39 different ways your data can be produced", but instead to think about the questions "that matter". Bene't considers that the trend is really what you should be looking for:

> Precision is not what you're after; it's all about the trend – daily, weekly, monthly. Are more/fewer people listening, is there more/less positive engagement, more/fewer shares and likes? The machines go in for a broad-brush approach, so if your target is narrow and limited don't bother with anything more than the free versions of monitoring tools, and maintain relationships old-school.

When it comes to social media:

> Many organisations appear to believe Social is closer to advertising or marketing than comms. It is vital to remember Social is a

two-way street; you have to listen and respond, no matter how inane some of the incoming is. You are not the only one telling stories online – your recipients are making their own stories at the same time. And everyone is watching/listening to them as well as to you. If they create a damaging story which is more compelling than yours – and you don't rebut very fast – you're on the back foot from the beginning. And sometimes they're telling your story better than you do – jump on it, use it, don't let their efforts go to waste.

During his career, Bene't has dealt with many crises. Social media has increased the demands for swift responses, and he suggests that "decisions need to be discussed, taken and implemented in less than three hours". Whilst tactics can help to buy the time needed, "quite serious decisions must be taken at faster speeds. And faster decisions can take you into even more debateable territory." He sees a danger-ous development in journalists no longer having to stand up a story: "the reporting of Twitter-storms and Social attacks constitutes a story in itself …. They can just report on the fact that some people believe XX has happened." For him, "that's another reason for you to be engaged with these audiences; traditional journalists are picking up their stories and context from you online as well as through the usual channels".

For instance, Michael McCain, CEO of Canadian firm Maple Leaf Foods, made a series of personal tweets on the corporate account decry-ing President Trump's approach to Iran following the shooting down of a Ukrainian airliner.[7] The tweets were certainly heartfelt and left no room for any misinterpretation. Replies to the tweet ranged from sup-port through to extreme criticism, but also some used it as an opportu-nity to revisit criticism of McCain and incidents that have hit Maple Leaf Foods in the past.

The organisation Canadian Business for Social Responsibility thought this was an approach that other businesses should adopt.[8] But what is clear is that there are potentially significant risks involved. There are those who may simply object to the comments. These people may or may not be important to the organisation. But is the potential of having to relive past failures or scandals likely to have adverse consequences as well?

The challenge for any leader making such statements is to ensure that all potential consequences have been considered and assessed and that the relevant media and social media teams have the ability to respond effectively, if needed. This is part risk assessment and partly about preparation.

> *Lesson – Think through online comments, and don't be blindsided by their instant and informal nature*

The real difficulties in terms of managing reputations come when a leader makes comments without any consideration.

It could easily be argued if that an organisation is to have a clear purpose, then statements of purpose from its leader should be encouraged almost regardless of the consequences. Ben & Jerry's UK chose to directly confront the policies of the UK government when it tweeted about migrants crossing the English Channel:[9]

> Hey @PritiPatel we think the real crisis is our lack of humanity for people fleeing war, climate change and torture. We pulled together a thread for you …
>
> People wouldn't make dangerous journeys if they had any other choice. The UK hasn't resettled any refugees since March, but wars and violence continue. What we need is more safe and legal routes
>
> People cannot be illegal. And, it is enshrined in the 1951 Refugee Convention that crossing a border "illegally" should not impact your asylum claim
>
> "Stronger" borders aren't the answer and only puts more lives at risk [link to a video]
>
> We know experts at organisations like @RefugeeAction want to talk solutions with Ministers, so why not have these conversations?
>
> Let's remember we're all human and have the same rights to life regardless of the country we happen to have been born in.
>
> and once more for the back: PEOPLE CANNOT BE ILLEGAL.

As can be imagined, there was a backlash from the government and individual MPs, but widespread support as well. This is a clear example of a company deliberately tackling an issue about which it feels strongly despite knowing what may happen. But it fits the approach of the company, which, after all, has a Head of Global Activism Strategy.[10]

Any individual has to appreciate that when they are posting on any social media, they are making a public comment. The usual excuses of being "young" or "having been on a journey" when past inappropriate posts are highlighted carry less and less weight. They may have worked for a while, but with Twitter having been founded in 2006 and Facebook in 2004, a lot of time has now passed. They have been part of everyday communications for a long time.

COVID-19

It is not possible to consider communications and reputation management without considering the issues related to coronavirus, COVID-19.

As soon as the seriousness of the virus became clear, those companies which had considered the implications realised the potential impact on their own operations and reputations. In such circumstances, any organisation faces a series of challenges and choices. The path of least resistance is simply to do what they are told, usually by government.

An alternative, and one that can help strengthen a reputation, is to be seen to be taking charge of the situation. The early stages of the virus crisis saw some very good examples of companies seizing the initiative and, as a result, gaining media coverage for their actions and praise from the public. In other words, strong, decisive action brought with it a boost to reputations.

Without being too sceptical about the intentions of organisations, the COVID-19 crisis provided an ideal opportunity for them to be very publicly seen to be doing the right thing and to be completely in tune with the priorities of the population, the media, governments and other stakeholders:

- Apple donated money and facemasks.
- Just East gave a discount for NHS workers.
- Uber gave 200,000 free rides to NHS staff and offered 100,000 free meals through Uber East.

- Krispy Kreme gave 50% off orders for emergency workers.
- Pret gave NHS workers free hot drinks and 50% off everything else.
- Costa Coffee and Caffè Nero both gave free hot drinks to NHS staff.
- McDonald's gave free drinks to NHS, council and emergency service staff.

Others, though, seemed to make complete misjudgements. Those involved will certainly have to regain the trust of many of their key audiences, not least customers in many cases. There has been talk of boycotts and long-lasting damage for those who appeared to misuse COVID-19 or not protect the most vulnerable from the impact of the pandemic. To quote a company chair quoted in *Retail Week*: "The modern shopper … will remember the retailers who helped them and their families and friends during the bad times".[11]

Airlines were amongst the first sectors to consider the impact on their businesses, suggesting that government support would be needed. Budget carrier easyJet warned that a number of airlines could even go bust. However, it paid out a £174 million dividend to its shareholders whilst also seeking support from the government. Speaking on the radio, its chief executive claimed that the company was legally obliged to make the pay-out.

Other stock market-listed companies though decided not to make such pay-outs, including the brewing company Shepherd Neame and housebuilders Crest Nicholson.

EasyJet appeared to compound the situation by trying to drastically change the working terms and conditions of staff. This led staff to present a petition against their own employers to the government.

But the approach also took on an internal dynamic when the founder of the company and largest shareholder, Sir Stelios Haji-Ioannou, criticised the leadership team, particularly the chief finance officer. He focused on the need to cancel an order for new aircraft, warning that otherwise the company would be unable to repay a government loan on time.

So the initial decisions turned into a very public discussion about the way in which the company should be run. Organisations need to keep in mind what the appetite and needs of the media, and other channels, are at any one time. Whilst the main focus continued to be on the health elements and societal demands of COVID-19, that did not mean there was no appetite for other stories. Some were happy to have a distraction. The national press liked to feature stories with a COVID-19 angle, but not always focused on the health elements. The easyJet story played directly into this narrative.

Similarly, Virgin Atlantic was at the forefront of pushing for a large bailout of the airline industry. But many questioned why Sir Richard Branson was not putting more money into the venture rather than asking for significant government support.

Eventually, the announcement came that he was investing more money in the Virgin Group, around $250 million. A personal blog post explained the seriousness with which Sir Richard took the situation:

> This is the most significant crisis the world has experienced in my lifetime. I usually think out loud and often share my every thought, but the scale and breadth of serious issues affecting our people and our businesses this week have meant this is the first chance I have had to put my thoughts down on paper.[12]

The blog read like a semi-apology, but showed that even the best minds, those who know the value of their own brand, can get things wrong. Sir Richard is no different.

Lesson — Reputations cannot be seen in isolation, they are part of wider social discussions

---

In one of the worst examples of a failure to understand the severity of a situation or its reputational impact, Britannia Hotels, which runs over 60 hotels across the UK, closed its hotel in Aviemore, Scotland and not only issued letters terminating the employment of staff, but also told them to leave their accommodation immediately. This left them with no job and nowhere to live. One of those losing their job decided to put a copy of the letter they received on social media. The ensuing outrage gained national coverage, and at least initially, the company did not comment. Eventually, it claimed that there had been an "administrative error", but without clarifying whether the staff would be reinstated or whether job losses would happen in other closed hotels across the chain. This was after Nicola Sturgeon, the First Minister of Scotland, said she "unreservedly" condemned the action; leading TV presenter Piers Morgan called it "contemptible"; former Deputy Leader of the Labour Party, Tom Watson, said he would "'never use" the chain again; and BBC broadcaster and journalist Andrew Neil tweeted:[13] "I suspect many folks, when they see this, will be adding Britannia Hotels to the list of businesses they will not be frequenting when this crisis is over."

In an obvious attempt to try to repair some of the damage done, the company let the government know that it would make space available for NHS workers in the hotels it had had to close as a result of the virus outbreak. However, employees then complained about ongoing job losses in the hotels which had closed.

Compare that with the actions of former Manchester United footballer Gary Neville, who simply opened his hotels free of charge to health workers to help in the battle against the virus.

A company that has long found the management of its reputation difficult is the sportswear retailer Sports Direct. The owner of the company, Mike Ashley, has long been unafraid to challenge accepted wisdom where it comes to his reputation as well.

During the time of the initial outbreak of COVID-19 in the UK, Sports Direct almost seemed to do everything it could to undermine its own credibility. Once the government announced a full lockdown, preventing non-essential shops from opening, Sports Direct initially announced that it would be staying open. After an online backlash, the company clarified that its stores would remain closed until told otherwise by government. Comments from government ministers made it very clear that the stores should remain closed.

Whilst that would normally be damaging enough, it then emerged that the company had doubled the prices of some of the brands it owns. It was also still making staff come to work even though the stores were closed, and for those on zero-hours contracts it was unclear whether they would be paid at all.[14]

Sports Direct was not alone in trying to be classified as an "essential" retailer – several electrical stores tried to ask the government whether they qualified as well. In the US, GameStop tried to make a similar claim.

But combined with its apparent attitude towards its staff, Sport Direct's approach seemed more about doing all it could to protect its business than anything else. Could Sports Direct argue that it was singled out for criticism more than others? Yes, it could. But this is where continuous offences against reputation come into play. Sports Direct had form, so that only amplified each poorly received action.

JD Wetherspoon, the pub chain, told its 40,000 staff that they would not be paid until the company had been reimbursed by the government under the support schemes for businesses that had been established. In response, Rachel Reeves MP, Chair of the Business, Energy and Industrial Strategy Select Committee, tweeted:[15]

> Unacceptable that Wetherspoons has refused to pay its 40,000 employees until it receives its Govt loan – potentially in late April – after first refusing to lock down altogether. If bosses disregard employees' wellbeing then Govt should take tougher action to force compliance.

Wetherspoons is another company with a high-profile leader in its chairman, Tim Martin. Martin was unafraid to be a leading voice championing Brexit and is regularly in the media. Following the company's decision, he received a letter signed by nearly 100 MPs complaining that:

> You employ 40,000 wonderful workers whose skills, hard work and enthusiasm are cherished by the country. They have also generated record profits for your company.
>
> However, Wetherspoons has fallen short in supporting these workers at a time of crisis. Allowing thousands of people to go penniless for a prolonged period of time is disgraceful.[16]

After receiving the letter, the company reversed its decision. However, it continued to be criticised for its failure to pay its supply chain.

Both companies received a letter from Reeves inviting them to explain how they were looking after their staff.

This led Ashley to release an extraordinary public "apology" in an open letter. Ashley is not a leader who backs down in the face of pressure. It is possible that the strength of the reaction left him with little choice, but he was also attempting to sell Newcastle United Football Club at the time as well. A poor reputation can impact price.

The letter said:[17]

> I thought it was necessary to address and apologise for much of what has been reported across various media outlets. ... I am deeply apologetic about the misunderstandings of the last few days. We will learn from this and will try not to make the same mistakes in the future.

In a typical "half-apology" approach often employed by those who don't really want to apologise, the open letter suggested an element of misreporting and misunderstanding, not poor decisions.

Lesson – The reputation of a leader impacts the organisation they lead

---

There were a great many, often tech, leaders who were only too willing to give their views on the impact of the coronavirus and gave the impression, some more clearly than others, that they worried more about the economic impact than the human impact.

Then add in those who appeared to have made fun of the virus and those suffering from it. The Harrods chief executive Michael Ward was filmed by his daughter pretending to struggle for breath and coughing. The video was posted on TikTok.[18]

The former Tottenham Hotspur and England footballer Dele Alli posted a video on Snapchat of him wearing a face mask before appearing to single out an Asian man, then moving to a bottle of antiseptic wash before a caption appeared saying: "This virus gunna have to be quicker than that to catch me[19]."

The Football Association and Alli's club immediately appreciated the damage the video was likely to do, and action was taken against him.

Many of these types of posts in themselves will not cause a downfall, but they do all chip away at reputations and credibility. We will have to wait to see whether the actions, easily promised on social media, to boycott certain companies because of their actions actually happen and have an impact.

Without doubt, though, many organisations, particularly companies, will have some ground to make up. Some may choose to focus on simply appealing to consumers through new products, better services or lower prices. But this assumes that the way they have dealt with the outbreak, or treated their staff and suppliers is, whilst not necessarily entirely forgotten, put to one side or outweighed by the offer of, say, a bargain.

This is taking a significant risk — a balanced risk in some of the cases. Others will simply have failed to think through the potential consequences. This short-term focus ignores, or underplays, the role that stakeholders play.

It also ignores what others in the "market" may do as well. Good practices or efforts will be rightly lauded by stakeholders, and poor practice called out. Are the organisations on the receiving end ready for that eventuality? Was that factored into their initial decisions?

> *Lesson — The consequences of your actions are played out in the behaviour and actions of your stakeholders*

The actions of Sports Direct or Wetherspoons will have made perfect sense in the narrow confines of the board room — decisions seemingly focused solely on what makes balance sheet sense, decisions that fail to think about anyone outside that board room. Such a decision-making environment is typically characterised by:

- Loud, dominant or influential figures.
- Limited discussion.
- A lack of effective decision-making.
- A lack of outside perspective.
- Decisions focused on "the numbers", but no other data or information.

Listening

There is, of course, a wealth of help and advice available to organisations about good governance and decision-making, so there should be no excuse. But more action is needed.

The Institute of Directors noted in its 2019 manifesto, designed to influence the programme of whichever political party was to win the coming UK general election, that there should be three broad objectives:

- Increase the accountability of the UK corporate governance system to stakeholders and wider society.
- Improve the competence and professionalism of UK board members – whose role is central to business decision-making.
- Enhance the ability of board members to pursue long-term, sustainable business behaviour – including addressing the challenge of climate change.[20]

This is the despite the work of the Financial Reporting Council (FRC), which exists to regulate accountants, auditors and actuaries, and operates the UK's corporate governance system. The FRC publishes the UK Corporate Governance Code, which states that: "The board should carry out a robust assessment of the company's emerging and principal risks."[21]

Only in the footnotes does it goes on to say:

> Principal risks should include, but are not necessarily limited to, those that could result in events or circumstances that might threaten the company's business model, future performance, solvency or liquidity and *reputation*. In deciding which risks are principal risks companies should consider the potential impact and probability of the related events or circumstances, and the timescale over which they may occur.[22] (italics added)

But when it comes to looking at executive pay and remuneration, it clearly states: "Remuneration arrangements should ensure *reputational* and other risks from excessive rewards, and behavioural risks that can arise from target-based incentive plans, are identified and mitigated."[23] (italics added)

When it comes to pay, it is very clear that the FRC as well as businesses are well aware of the specific reputational risks that arise. It is so special that it is worth a mention. Whilst, of course, it is not possible for such principles to list every issue that a business has to consider, it is interesting to note that remuneration seems to be a special case. It is quite possible that the next time the Code is revised, climate change may be included for special consideration as well.

Pay and remuneration may continue to be a "hot button" topic for many, and there is no doubt that the media retains a keen interest, but expectations move on. One of the consequences of COVID-19 appears to be that a keener interest is being taken in the welfare of employees and that "fringe" issues such as disparities in pay are entering the mainstream.

Since April 2017, employers in the UK with at least 250 workers have been required to publish details about their gender pay gap. There was also consideration of extending this to smaller firms and potentially enhancing enforcement powers. The problem so far is that despite the data being published, the gap remains largely the same.[24]

> Lesson – Listen to your those challenging you, your opponents – they often lead the agenda

If you want to see a direct opposite of the Martin/Ashley school of leadership and reputation, then take a look at the Chief Executive of BP, Bernard Looney. BP is itself an organisation that has had to take a large number of reputational hits.

One of Looney's first actions upon taking over the role was to announce that the company was going to be "re-inventing" itself and would be net zero by 2050 or sooner. It is not the first company to make such a commitment, but given the nature of its sector, this appears highly ambitious. Looney's own comment is quite striking: "The world's carbon budget is finite and running out fast; we need a rapid transition to net zero."[25]

This was an early statement of intent, but Looney also seemed like a thoroughly modern chief executive. He has a beautifully constructed LinkedIn profile,[26] introduced himself on Instagram, promised to "talk openly", and mentioned how he considers "open and honest discussion crucial". A video on Instagram on day one of a visit to the team in Germany was used to demonstrate this openness and, as was doubtless part of the strategy, it made him look human.

Considering this approach in the context of reputation building, then, it is about:

- Making a clear break with the past.
- Establishing a new type of leadership.
- Getting ahead of the most pressing issues.
- Communicating directly with relevant external stakeholders.
- Communicating directly with internal stakeholders, such as employees working in many countries across the world.

BP is an oil company, and as its critics would say, a planet-destroying fossil fuel company. Not that you would know that from its corporate website, where it says it "deliver[s] heat, light and mobility products and services to people all around the world in ways that will help to drive the transition to a lower carbon future".

But as Greenpeace states:

> Our world runs on oil – you could even say we're addicted to it. But using all this oil is causing climate change and threatening our future. Oil companies are also taking huge risks to reach dwindling supplies and ignoring the rights of Indigenous Peoples. Around the world, people are standing up to these companies with a single message: no more oil.[27]

As a new chief executive, addressing head-on the single biggest challenge facing the company set the right tone for Looney's leadership and what he wants to achieve. In the same way that a newly elected president or prime minister will expend their political capital on the tougher decisions right at the start, the same can be said of the business capital of new executives. They have the chance to take big decisions right at the start. They otherwise face distractions from other matters coming to the fore or being pushed off track by outside pressure.

This does not mean that activists are stepping back from challenging BP and Looney. Indeed, the tone of Greenpeace's response to the announcement was sceptical, to say the least, suggesting a lack of promised actions and that all the difficult decisions were being pushed off into the future.

Grandiose statements will rightly attract media coverage, and politicians may come out in support, but they do not replace the need for action. In many ways, they make the need for action even more pressing – the big words need to be backed up with big actions. The words help to attract additional attention. By setting your own standards and hurdles, you are certainly more in control of the agenda, but you have nowhere to hide if delivery is not forthcoming.

This has to be seen in the context of what other companies are doing as well. Microsoft, for example, will be carbon-negative by 2030, and by 2050 it will remove from the environment all the carbon the company has emitted, either directly or by electrical consumption, since it was founded in 1975.

British American Tobacco (BAT) has committed to making all its direct operations carbon-neutral by 2030. Of all the sectors suffering from reputational challenges, there is arguably none bigger than tobacco. BAT has for many years tried to grab the corporate social responsibility (CSR) agenda and use it to improve its reputation. Some activists accuse companies of "greenwashing", spinning what they are doing to deceive the public so that they look better. But the likes of BAT genuinely pushed CSR forward and were early adopters, for instance, of external, independent validation of their actions.

For organisations with reputation issues, being at the forefront of environmental concerns is a way of recovering from some of the historic damage and moving to a much more positive outlook. They may, if persuaded with sufficient rigour and vigour, be leaders in the green movement and act as an example to others.

However, this means being prepared to:

1) Be transparent – open to scrutiny and question.
2) Be reflective – if the agenda fails, then reassessing and learning the lessons.
3) Be a champion – adopting a public profile that shouts loudly.

Reverse ferret

Some organisations are nimble enough to appreciate when they make an error and reverse it quickly. Take the example of Liverpool Football Club

(LFC).[28] But even having a fanatical worldwide support base and vocal former players in prominent positions across the media failed to protect the club when it announced that it was to furlough some non-playing staff during the COVID-19 lockdown.

Former captain Jamie Carragher tweeted: "Jurgen Klopp [LFC's manager] showed compassion for all at the start of this pandemic, senior players heavily involved in @Premier League players taking wage cuts. Then all that respect and goodwill is lost – poor this, @LFC".[29] Former striker Stan Collymore tweeted: "I don't know of any Liverpool fan of any standing that won't be anything other than disgusted at the club for furloughing staff. It's just plain [expletive] wrong".[30]

Fan groups and others also led the criticism, which was covered widely across the media as well. As is often the case, there seemed to be no single cause for the outcry. Instead, it was a combination of reasons, such as:

- Other leading clubs continuing to keep non-playing staff on 100% of wages.
- Seeming to go against well-received measures, including the club offering stewards to help with crowds at supermarkets.
- Earlier criticism by the government of "rich" football clubs not contributing sufficiently to the COVID-19 fight.

But cutting across all of this was the introduction of a measure that undermined the reputation of a club that prides itself on being part of the community. Liverpool is a city that has taken a lot of knocks over the years, not least economically. The move seemed completely at odds with the whole concept of supporting its local community, not least economically.

Within a short space of time, Chief Executive Officer Peter Moore issued an open letter to Liverpool supporters reversing the club's decision:

> We believe we came to the wrong conclusion last week to announce that we intended to apply to the Coronavirus Retention Scheme and furlough staff due to the suspension of the Premier League football calendar, and are truly sorry for that.[31]

Such an episode illustrates the need for any organisation to understand what makes up its reputation in the first place. It should be the focus of any decisions made. It is all too easy to make comments about what an organisation stands for and means without those being engrained in everything the organisation does.

The LFC example demonstrates that organisations have choices when they make a decision that leads to a backlash or adverse reaction:

1) Live by it – stick with the decision and double down.
2) Consider a review – announce a move to look again at the decision.
3) Reverse the decision – look for a form of words that tries to repair some of the immediate damage.

None of these options is without its pitfalls. A quick reversal may take the immediate pressure off, but it may just delay the pain and damage. In the case of LFC, Moore's letter mentioned the "inevitable damage" of the COVID-19 crisis. The financial hit to the club is going to have to be dealt with, but the form will now change.

"Toughing it out" may initially seem like the least preferable option, but explaining a decision, how it was arrived at and its clear benefits can bring with it significant benefits. A strengthening of leadership can be demonstrated, along with a belief in the decision itself. Being easily dissuaded too quickly can itself inflict more damage and lead to questions about the quality of leadership.

> *Lesson – Take a deep breath and reappraise, then if confident, double down*

So how can the best course of action be decided?

To pretend there is one easy option would be to mislead. Rather, this comes down to the quality of the initial decision-making process. As LFC showed, mistakes are always possible even when good processes and motives are in place.

Think instead of asking yourself a series of questions:

1) Where the right people involved in the decision-making?
2) Were all the relevant issues considered and, critically, balanced? Even if the immediate focus was on the finances of the organisation,

were the legal, HR, and communications elements considered as well?

3) Were all the other options considered, and in balanced way? Ensure that there was not a favoured option or one championed above and beyond others from the outset.
4) Were the potential views of key stakeholder groups factored in?
5) Was the "what happens if this announcement goes wrong" scenario considered?

Considering the downsides, balancing the risks, and examining all the options not only makes for better decisions, but also makes the decisions more defendable if they come under scrutiny.

Lesson – Organisations often contribute to their own crises

What all this points to is a lesson that for the most part, organisations create – or at the very least, contribute to – their own crises and the damage inflicted on their reputations. Not having the necessary evidence and data available or making decisions without access to the full range of advice needed leads to sub-optimal decision-making. Or put another way, the risks are not fully identified and addressed.

Of course, there is always a danger that the unexpected can happen. No organisation can ever claim to be 100% immune from crises or to have successfully managed every risk. But if the worst does happen, then every organisation needs to be able to outline, in a meaningful and comprehensive way, its decision-making process.

This would include how the full range of views, such as those of staff and their representatives, have been included. We have all seen examples where the main criticism of the behaviour of an organisation comes from internal audiences. That is often a result of not having processes in place whereby a genuine dialogue with teams can take place, or where the structures exist but nothing is done with the information received. Pretending to listen is almost worse than not listening at all.

It is always worth considering having to explain such a position in the event of a crisis. Here, the allegation would be that the problem had been raised through formal channels, but you did nothing about it.

Those at board level might suggest that the information never made it through to them. If they were unaware, then there was nothing to address as far as they were concerned. That is a position, but it is a poor one. Why? If there is a failure to report, then that comes down to a system failure, which ultimately the leaders are directly responsible for. Trying to deflect from one failing simply opens up another line of attack.

Everything is public

You should always consider that every email, internal memo and conversation is potentially public. The idea that anything is "secret" or "for internal purposes only" is increasingly unrealistic. Action should always be taken where it comes to IT and security matters. To do otherwise would be negligent, and could well leave you open to regulatory intervention and significant fines.

But even with the best systems in place, you cannot remove the human element. People keep documents, print them off, email them to others and keep their own records even if they should not be doing so.

The chances of such documents becoming public are increased when grievances are not addressed or voices are consistently not listened to. This builds up ill will which can then seep out through the media or online.

Of course, legal action can be threatened, and that will work in some instances. Think, however, through the lens of a reputation. If you make a threat of legal action, then you need to be prepared to see it through. A hollow threat will only serve to embolden the media or opponents. Rather than demonstrating strength, it shows weakness. Threats not followed through make for an even better media story.

This is not to say that the law cannot play a valuable role – it can, and it does. But always come back to a full analysis of what may happen, the risks involved, and what they may do to your reputation. Even if a legal challenge is the right course of action and completely justified, could you stand the reputational hit of it being portrayed in a "David versus Goliath"-type battle?

If a legal challenge is the chosen course, then organisations need to consider the role communications can play in supporting it.

Fill the void

The modern media is full of stories drawn largely or exclusively from social media. Stories are often supported by quotes lifted from social media, particularly Twitter. Those voices and opinions are often not from experts, but from those with a strong opinion who can articulate themselves within a small character limit or in a thread that makes for essential reading.

> *Lesson – Stakeholders make correct decisions, but often based on incorrect information available to them*

Every audience looks online for information – journalists researching stories, elected representatives and their teams in advance of meetings, customers looking to make a purchase decision, the list goes on.

The lesson is that organisations need to ensure that they do everything they can to control the information in circulation about them.

Any stakeholder will make judgements and decisions based on the information available to them. It is not necessarily their fault if it is not available to them or they only have access to incorrect, partial or misleading information.

This brings us, in part, back to the option highlighted earlier about sticking with a decision and doubling down on it. One of the reasons why this approach can be so difficult is that the sharing of information can be a difficult call. What information should be shared, and what can be shared? Audiences may be asked to take decision-making partly on trust. But trust, as we have seen, is often in short supply – especially for those with already poor reputations.

There is a circular argument here, but audiences are more likely to trust decisions if they already have trust in the organisation making the decisions. You have to build trust and your reputation in advance of making tough decisions.

If you are unable to share much information regarding the decision but the trust is there, then audiences may accept this. If the reputation and trust are not there, then the lack of information will be greeted with increased scepticism.

My assertion throughout this book is that organisations should always have an eye on their reputation. But you can make even more of an argument for building a reputation if you know that some big decisions are coming up. If you need audiences to have faith in those decisions and in the leadership of your organisation, then put the reputational effort in now in order to build it up for those more challenging times to come.

Notes

1 Campbell (2016) (www.prweek.com/article/1386983/alastair-campbell-reputation-not-media).
2 Kantar (2019).
3 Urbanski (2017) (www.linkedin.com/pulse/best-government-campaigns-linkedin-jennifer-urbanski/).
4 Urbanski (2018) (www.linkedin.com/pulse/how-use-linkedin-like-pm-trudeau-jennifer-urbanski/).
5 *The Guardian* (2020) (www.youtube.com/watch?v=jmSPOSGpAYs).
6 Hannaford (2020) (www.gq-magazine.co.uk/politics/article/dr-li-wenliang-death).
7 Maple Leaf Foods, tweet, 13 January 2020 (https://twitter.com/MapleLeafFoods/status/1216529698433437696).
8 See CBC News (2020) www.cbc.ca/news/canada/new-brunswick/maple-leaf-foods-ceo-michael-mccain-twitter-comments-1.5427178).
9 Ben & Jerry's UK, tweet, 11 August 2020 (https://twitter.com/benandjerrysuk/status/1293214277621489666).
10 For an interview with Christopher Miller, who holds the position, see Deighton (2020).
11 Latham (2020) (www.veracitysearch.co.uk/insights/2020/3/4/coronavirus-compassion-or-callousness).
12 Branson (2020) (www.virgin.com/richard-branson/my-response-global-crisis).
13 Andrew Neil, tweet, 20 March 2020 (https://twitter.com/afneil/status/1240895962144550914).
14 Butler, Wood and Murphy (2020) (www.theguardian.com/business/2020/mar/24/mike-ashley-sports-direct-bows-to-pressure-and-closes-stores-coronavirus).
15 Rachel Reeves, tweet, 24 March 2020 (https://twitter.com/rachelreevesmp/status/1242397983682985987).
16 Clive Lewis MP, Facebook post, 25 March 2020 (www.facebook.com/labour-clivelewis/photos/ive-joined-other-mps-in-signing-a-letter-demanding-the-jd-wetherspoon-pub-chain-/2847464425330346/).
17 See www.pressreader.com/uk/the-chronicle-9c96/20200328/281573767791448.
18 See Thompson (2020) (www.dailymail.co.uk/news/article-8134309/Harrods-chief-executive-appears-mock-coronavirus-sufferers.html).

19 See Guardian Football (2020) (www.youtube.com/watch?v=ldx41eOH6uE).
20 Institute of Directors (2019) (www.iod.com/Portals/0/PDFs/Campaigns%20 and%20Reports/Corporate%20Governance/IoD%20Manifesto%20- %20Corporate%20Governance.pdf?ver=2019-11-19-082215-783).
21 Financial Reporting Council (2018) (www.frc.org.uk/getattachment/88bd8c45 -50ea-4841-95b0-d2f4f48069a2/2018-UK-Corporate-Governance-Code-FINAL .pdf).
22 Ibid.
23 Ibid.
24 Treasury Select Committee (2019) (http://data.parliament.uk/writtenevidence/ committeeevidence.svc/evidencedocument/treasury-committee/effectiveness -of-gender-pay-gap-reporting/oral/102805.html).
25 BP (2020) (www.bp.com/en/global/corporate/news-and-insights/press-releases /bernard-looney-announces-new-ambition-for-bp.html).
26 For a full examination of his profile, see Szomszor (2020) (www.linkedin .com/pulse/how-new-bp-ceo-demonstrating-connected-leadership-social -szomszor/).
27 Greenpeace (n.d.) (www.greenpeace.org.uk/challenges/oil-drilling-and-pipelines/).
28 For full disclosure, I must admit to being a very long-term supporter of the club.
29 Jamie Carragher, tweet, 4 April 2020 (https://twitter.com/carra23/status /1246467781681451008).
30 Stan Collymore, tweet, 4 April 2020 (https://twitter.com/stancollymore/status /1246468473678630918).
31 Liverpool Football Club (2020) (www.liverpoolfc.com/news/announcements /392368-a-letter-from-peter-moore-to-liverpool-supporters).

References

Alastair Campbell, 'Reputation is not all about the media any more', *PR Week*, 11 March 2016.

Alex Hannaford, 'The last days of Dr Li Wenliang, the Chinese coronavirus whistleblower', *GQ*, 16 March 2020.

BP, 'BP sets ambition for net zero by 2050, fundamentally changing organisation to deliver', Media Release, 12 February 2020.

CBC News, 'Business group urges companies to follow Michael McCain's lead after anti-Trump tweets', 14 January 2020 (www.cbc.ca/news/ canada/new-brunswick/maple-leaf-foods-ceo-michael-mccain-twitter -comments-1.5427178).

Financial Reporting Council, *The UK Corporate Governance Code*, July 2018.

Greenpeace, 'Oil drilling and pipelines', n.d. (https://www.greenpeace.org .uk/challenges/oil-drilling-and-pipelines/).

Guardian Football, 'Tottenham's Dele Alli apologies over coronavirus video: "It wasn't funny"', 10 February 2020 (www.youtube.com/watch?v=ldx 41eOH6uE).

Institute of Directors, *IoD Manifesto: Corporate Governance*, 2019.

Jennifer Urbanski, 'The best government campaigns on LinkedIn', *LinkedIn*, 18 April 2017.

Jennifer Urbanski, 'How to use LinkedIn like PM Trudeau', *LinkedIn*, 1 February 2018.

Kantar, 'Authentic communication in a mistrusting world: Reaching consumers online and offline', April 2019.

Kate Latham, 'Coronavirus: Compassion or callousness?', *Veracity Search*, 3 April 2020.

Katie Deighton, 'Ben & Jerry's activism chief on fighting for the causes currently being neglected', *The Drum*, 23 April 2020.

Liverpool Football Club, *A Letter for Peter Moore to Liverpool Supporters*, 6 April 2020.

Phil Szomszor, 'How the new BP CEO is demonstrating connected leadership with social media', *LinkedIn*, 13 February 2020.

Paul Thompson, 'Harrods boss "mocks coronavirus victims" as he coughs and says "I'm gonna die!" in shocking TikTok video', *MailOnline*, 20 March 2020 (www.dailymail.co.uk/news/article-8134309/Harrods -chief-executive-appears-mock-coronavirus-sufferers.html).

Sarah Butler, Zoe Wood, and Simon Murphy, 'Sports direct staff facing uncertain future after pressure forces store closures', *The Guardian*, 24 March 2020.

Sir Richard Branson, 'My response to the global crisis', *Blog*, 21 March 2020.

The Guardian, 'Coronavirus: Nurse in tears after panic buying leaves shelves empty of food, YouTube', 20 March 2020.

Treasury Select Committee, 'The effectiveness of gender pay gap reporting, HC 2240', *Oral Evidence Session*, 5 June 2019.

4

THE CHARITY CHALLENGE

Charities are at the cutting edge of reputation management. Too often, reputation management is considered the preserve of corporates, but in reality, the stakeholder pressures on charities mean that reputation management is, or should be, at the top of their priority list.

Many leaders often work with a range of organisations. Successful business leaders can find themselves leading charities as well. They get involved because of their valuable commercial experience, and this discipline can be extremely useful. However, it often seems like the reputation lessons they consider in the business setting get lost when they start working for a charity.

It is almost as if they do not believe that the "normal rules" of reputation management apply to charities, but that couldn't be any further from the truth.

DOI: 10.4324/9781003293880-5

> *Lesson – Reputations are not just about consumer-facing businesses*

There is no doubt that the charity sector has come under increasing pressure in recent years. The stories come thick and fast concerning everything from misbehaving chief executives through to matters related to fundraising. In a 2014 survey of the voluntary sector, 90% of charities said they felt that the sector had become subject to more media interest and scrutiny.[1]

For a long time, charities were perceived as having a special pass when it came to their reputation. The media always focused on corporate misbehaviour and did not appear very interested in what charities were getting up to. That has changed, partly as a consequence of corporates cleaning up their acts, but at the same time, charities have become financially larger, more part of everyday life (as they provide services), often have high-profile executives, undertake more campaigning, take their fundraising more seriously and have reached out beyond traditional supporters etc. Charities have changed.

As the nature of charities has changed, so has their profile. That higher profile has brought with it adverse media and political comment that many charities did not see coming. This was an unexpected consequence, and meant that the issue of reputation management had to be taken seriously.

> *Lesson – Apply the same reputation "rules" regardless of sector or organisation type*

Speaking about the challenges faced by charities, Gemma Holding, CEO of Cancer Support UK said:

> I think charities *absolutely* face particular reputational challenges – challenges that do not apply as acutely as in other sectors. For example, I have yet to hear a person say that they are "no longer prepared to shop with John Lewis" as they recently a bad customer experience at Tesco. As absurd as this sounds, this attitude

does seem to apply to charities. The negative actions of one charity really can affect the reputation of other entirely unrelated charities – and the sector as a whole. With this in mind, it is up to all of us to protect the reputation of the sector as a whole and not simply protect our own interests. Individuals need to be brave and challenge issues head-on, even when leaving a complicated organisation may seem like the easier option. The Cancer Recovery Foundation had had five CEOs in the six years before I joined– this would suggest, to me at least, that I was not the only CEO appointed who came across issues that had potential for reputational damage. However, unless someone takes a stand and challenges bad practice in the sector, it will inevitably affect us all further down the line.

And this points to an issue that makes charities just that little bit different. Certainly, each charity has its own reputation to worry about, but there is also a heightened sense of collective reputation, regardless of which sector they actually operate in.

A research report by the Charity Commission, the charity regulator, Trust in Charities, 2018, found that "Public trust in charities has plateaued since 2016".

Charities still enjoy a large amount of trust, but when it is damaged, the impact always appears worse. For a charity, it seems that the level of expectation is higher. But these expectations are often unrealistic. Charities, it appears, cannot:

- Pay "too much" in wages.
- Spend "too much" on fundraising.
- Spend money on support activities – advertising, communications etc.
- Have financial reserves of any significance.
- Spend on anything other than those they are raising funds for.

This makes operating in the charity sector fundamentally different.

As the same report states:

Charities have a special status in society, which comes with certain privileges (financial and reputational) and advantages (public support). With these advantages come obligations to act to a high standard of compliant and ethical behaviour that the public expects.

The charity sector has suffered some significant crises in recent years, including Kids Company, Oxfam, Save the Children and Age UK, which we consider in this chapter.

If there is any small comfort, then it is that charities are still trusted more than banks, MPs and private companies, but reports of distrust in charities continue to rise. Those aged 18–24 are more likely to trust charities than those aged 55 or over.

There is also a level of expectation regarding transparency in the distribution of funds and the end impact of charities' spending. This warranted because there are worries about the proportion of donations that reach the charities' intended beneficiaries.

Trust decreases when charities lack good financial stewardship, do not live their values and fail to have an impact. However, trust is protected when they deliver on these.

Fundamentally, trust matters to donations: 52% of those whose trust has increased say they donate more as a result, but 41% say they donate less when trust decreases.[2] A charity's reputation positively influences financial performance, and vice versa.[3]

Research consultancy nfpSynergy found in 2017 that charities were the fifth most trusted public institutions, behind the NHS, armed forces, police and schools.

Talking to me about the reputation challenges facing charities, Kirsty McHugh, a charity chief executive, explained:

> Having worked cross-sector, I strongly believe that charities face a particularly acute set of challenges in terms of reputation – to put it bluntly, they need to keep everybody happy – funders and donors, government and regulators, staff and general public – all this against a backdrop of a fight for funds, often against increasing need.
>
> Reputationally, this is a minefield. On one hand, it appears that public perception of charities is that they should primarily be volunteer-led and not pay attractive salaries to staff. On the other, there is a requirement that services delivered (often to the most

vulnerable in society) are high-quality – to fail on that has high reputational risk, quite aside from the human cost. Similarly, charities are acutely aware that where their funds come from can be under public scrutiny. However, I rarely meet a charity which didn't struggle with covering overheads and core costs – a rich donor would be a Godsend to many.

I am particularly interested in the perception of potential donors. Why do some of our richest individuals in society give least? The Centre for London's 2018 report on philanthropy (www.centrefor-london.org/publication/more-better-together-giving-london/) indicates that the ultra-wealthy give just £240 p.a. There are a wide range of reasons for these, which entities like the Philanthropy Collective, are exploring, but one of the issues seems to be about the reputation of the charity sector as somehow inefficient. This is ridiculous. I'm not sure if validated data exists, but I strongly suspect productivity per staff member in the charity sector would outstrip that of the private or public sectors. However, just a few high-profile media stories, combined with some old-fashioned views about what the charity sector is and does, have done damage.

Good reputation management is about thinking ahead. What's the worst that could happen to you and how would you respond? Be honest: what are your weak points? And make sure that you address them and/or can justify them. If you accept money from those with a High Net Worth (HNW) or corporates, do you have an up-to-date ethical fundraising policy in place which people can actually use, rather than merely place in a computer file and trot out for statutory funders? If you're staff, when do you escalate to trustees, and are your trustees equipped to make informed, balanced decisions? Are you also using your political nous as well as following the letter of your fundraising policies? Sometimes things can be justified on paper, but it just doesn't feel right. Don't ignore that feeling – it's often right.

We will see many of these factors playing out in some of the major crises that have faced charities in recent years.

For charities in England and Wales, reputations are constantly under scrutiny. The Charity Commission places a heavy emphasis on the need for charities to protect their reputations.

In its guidance for charity trustees, it suggests that a charity's resources must be managed responsibly and that trustees must "avoid exposing the charity's assets, beneficiaries or reputation to undue risk".[4]

The guidance goes on to give some examples of where such reputation damage can be inflicted, for instance when trustees are thinking about how the charity will obtain funds.

"It's difficult to lump all charities into one group given the varied nature of the sector," believes James White, head of campaigns at a number of larger charities:

> The ways charities are structured and governed, in particular the dynamic between Trustees and the Senior Leadership Team, is one area that could cause problems.
>
> The ways that charities are funded can also give rise to problems. The pressure to diversify sources of income might cause some charities to accept donations (or other support) from external sources or enter into commercial partnerships with profit-making entities that may result in tough questions being asked of the charity.
>
> The actions of individual employees, particularly for charities working with vulnerable people, can bring the entire organisation into disrepute.
>
> Whilst all of these issues (mismanagement, poor decision-making, rogue employees) can happen in any organisation, given the way that charities are, in the main, viewed in a positive light by the British public, any scandals have a tendency to resonate more loudly.

If a charity has an incident that could inflict reputational harm, then it is meant to make a Serious Incident Report (SIR) to the Charity Commission. What constitutes a serious enough level of harm is unclear, but many charities prefer to err on the side of caution and make a SIR under most circumstances. It may not, for instance, be clear at the very outset that reputational harm is coming their way. It can grow and build over a period of time, as it can for any type of organisation.

The Charity Commission can take action, and expects trustees to have avoided "exposing their charity to undue risk" and that they "should take reasonable steps to assess and manage risk to its activities, beneficiaries, property and reputation".[5]

You can start to see from this that reputation is at the heart of how a charity should be run, and if sufficient steps are not taken to protect it, then regulatory action is possible.

Speaking about the protection of reputations, then Chief Executive of the Charity Commission Sam Younger said: "Our advice is to get your defence in first. Be your own critical friend. Ask yourself how you will explain your decision to beneficiaries, the public, or a journalist".[6]

Some charities benefit by being focused on "popular" issues, ones that attract public sympathy and support. Others operate in challenging sectors and may deal with groups that do not always elicit the same reaction. They always have to work that much harder when it comes to their reputations.

According to James White:

> charities are seen as trustworthy, and are felt to be acting in the interest of their beneficiaries. Anything that a charity does needs to be in accordance with those two principles. If a charity sticks to this approach, they won't go too far wrong!

Sadly, there have been many high-profile examples of this seeming to go wrong.

E.ON and Age UK

Age UK worked with the energy firm E.ON in developing an energy tariff designed for the elderly. The charity was heavily criticised after it came to light that it had been paid £6 million a year by Eon for promoting the tariff. The heart of the issue was not so much the payments or the relationship, but the nature of the tariff itself, which was not the cheapest available in the market or even the cheapest available from E.ON.

The initial arguments centred on whether the tariff offered the best value for pensioners. According to E.ON, it was the cheapest when launched, and E.ON suggested that customers could shift between tariffs. Age UK focused on the long-term certainty and stability the tariff offered the elderly. Its argument was quite nuanced, whereas those criticising the scheme could simply point to the costs. It did not help that Age UK itself had campaigned on high energy price tariffs.

The pressure led to E.ON abolishing the tariff and replacing it with a new version.

As is often the case in such circumstances, adverse media comment led to statements from senior politicians and a subsequent regulatory investigation. This is a familiar pattern which demonstrates that when it comes to communicating, especially in a crisis, all stakeholders need to be engaged.

All too often, crisis management is focused on media and social media comments, the ability to respond quickly and having senior personnel available to talk. However, the real longer-term and lasting damage comes from the fallout with other stakeholders, especially politicians.

The Charity Commission criticised Age UK for failing to be clear about the nature of the commercial relationship, and said that any fees or commission received need to be transparent: "Consider the risks and benefits to the charity's name and reputation of a commercial partnership and ensure that a charity's name and assets are valued and protected".[7]

> Lesson – Ask yourself whether the relationship makes reputational sense

Save the Children

In 2018, the charity faced allegations of child abuse and of senior staff paying for sex in Haiti. The initial crisis revealed sexual harassment allegations from 2012 and 2015 against senior team members. There then followed a focus on workplace relationships and claims of intimidation. It was revealed that a former chief executive of the charity had resigned for sending inappropriate text messages to several female employees. There had been investigations by the charity's trustees, which they admitted "should not have been left".[8] According to BBC reports, almost one in five staff at the charity claimed to have experienced harassment or discrimination.[9]

The charity found itself on the receiving end of near constant media attention and a regulatory investigation by the Charity Commission, and new funding applications to government were stopped.

Chief Executive Kevin Watkins used an interview with the *Financial Times* to set out his strategy to focus "frontline" resources on three themes: child survival, including tackling preventable diseases; supporting education; and ensuring child protection in countries hit by conflict.[10] These sorts of messages were very much designed to reassure the charity's donors, staff and volunteers – three key stakeholders.

Describing the crisis, the *Financial Times* suggested that Watkins had, as his "first response", apologised "unreservedly" to those affected. He then announced an independent review of the charity's workplace culture, appointed an external chair, and promised to publish the findings – all textbook responses. He did, though, go further, and delivered a programme to promote a change in management culture. This was a useful addition to the outcome which could be used in a public way to demonstrate to stakeholders that real action had been taken.

Another way organisations try to defend themselves is to widen the blame, suggesting that whilst they may have been the ones to have been caught, the practices are widespread. In this case, the interview mentioned "broader scrutiny of the sector" and how Save the Children had been helping to address "wider concerns over safeguarding in the aid sector".

This sort of positioning tries to grasp the reforming zeal and place the organisation at the head of finding a solution and delivering change. Where once it was part of the problem, now it is solving it.

Such incidents also demonstrate that trying to brush issues under the carpet or dealing with them in a very "quiet" way only makes the problem worse when it does come to light. It will invariably come to light, so the impact, and reputational damage, will be even more dramatic and serious.

Lesson – Take time to reflect on previous decisions

Oxfam

Oxfam was also one of the big international charities that, in the words of the Charity Commission, allowed a "culture of poor behaviour" to take root. The charity sought to cover up misconduct by senior aid workers in Haiti. An investigation by *The Times* found that aid workers had been dismissed or allowed to resign over their use of prostitutes, yet the charity did not inform the authorities properly.[11] The most damaging revelations were that the age of the prostitutes could not be established and some of the aid workers went on to work for other aid agencies who were not informed of the issue. Similar allegations were published related to Oxfam workers in Chad.

The chief executive of the charity resigned, Haiti banned it from operating in the country, high-profile celebrity supporters resigned, and the UK government cut the public money paid to it. With financial concerns looming, staff numbers were cut. But, like Save the Children, these were not the only problems faced by the charity. Oxfam also established an independent commission to consider allegations of bullying and discrimination. It found a "toxic work environment".

The actor Minnie Driver, who had been working with the charity for more than 20 years and was an ambassador, cut her ties. Archbishop Desmond Tutu retired as an ambassador with a statement saying:

> Archbishop Emeritus Desmond Tutu has supported Oxfam International's good work for many years, most recently as one of its global ambassadors.
>
> The Archbishop is deeply disappointed by allegations of immorality and possible criminality involving humanitarian workers linked to the charity.
>
> He is also saddened by the impact of the allegations on the many thousands of good people who have supported Oxfam's righteous work.[12]

Oxfam's corporate partnerships also came under serious pressure as a consequence. Only Waterstones gave a more unequivocal backing to Oxfam, and most of the other partners preferred to reserve judgement.

Such corporate supporters of any organisation are keenly aware of the implications for their own reputations. Being closely associated with any organisation that has behaved in a way that is incompatible with their own values or ethics can spell disaster for them. There is a need to show that this sort of behaviour is unacceptable, and that could have ramifications for the relationship.

Some may choose to very quickly put an end to the relationship, which would demonstrate in the clearest possible way that the offending behaviour is unacceptable to them. That would seem like the most straightforward response, but is it the best response?

1. Does the partner have all the facts, or would ending the relationship be premature?
2. If it turns out that the initial allegations are untrue or there was at least more nuance involved, could the immediate reaction rebound and hit the partner's reputation?
3. Is there potentially more to be gained by maintaining the relationship and helping the organisation through its difficulties?
4. Could ending the relationship deliver a backlash against the partner?

The responses to these types of questions will be different for each relationship, and may well depend on its strength, longevity and the reasons for being involved in the first place. That helps to explain why Waterstones was more supportive in its initial response, whereas other partners at least sought to buy themselves some more time, for instance to look at the outcome of investigations, before making any decision. There is also the possibility that a later decision to end a relationship will be less interesting to the media. Ending it immediately may contribute to the crisis, whereas leaving it until later may generate less interest and have a lower media impact, if any at all.

As far as Oxfam's recovery is concerned, it is critical for any organisation to work clearly and transparently to address problems. That approach has to include everything from media statements through to working collaboratively with any investigations. Once the results of investigations are released, then rather than quibbling over details of the report or minor aspects, the approach has to be one of accepting the recommendations and getting on with a plan to deliver them. Such a plan would ideally be drawn up with the help of outside experts and then published alongside a clear timetable for delivery. This means that the organisation can be held to account by a range of stakeholders and it can keep them up to date on developments. More regular communication can be a way of rebuilding trust. If a certain milestone cannot be met or a setback is encountered, then rather hiding it, it should be addressed head-on.

Trust in Oxfam has been rising since the initial scandal because of the changes that were implemented. It takes time, effort and transparency, but will eventually mean its reputation will be rebuilt. Maintaining the support of the likes of Glastonbury Festival has been critical. Having the Oxfam logo once again displayed prominently at the festival not only gave it global exposure, but also associated it with some of the biggest music acts in the world. That all contributes to the rebuilding process. Oxfam's scandal hit the value of its reputation, so rebuilding was needed.

A Charity Commission report into Oxfam found that: "Focusing on avoiding negative or critical media coverage when incidents have happened will not fulfil the trustees' duty to protect a charity's reputation, nor serve the shared responsibility to uphold the reputation of charity as a whole".[13]

Responding to the findings, the President of the Chartered Institute of Public Relations (CIPR) at the time, Emma Leech, summed up the challenge:

> Reputations are earned and maintained through effective operations that are managed with integrity and openness. Putting media coverage ahead of governance duties and moral responsibilities is always going to be more damaging than doing the right thing, however disruptive it may have been.

But she also set down a challenge to those in communications:

> Public relations professionals have a role in challenging such decisions, by bringing the perspective of the outside world into the organisation and reflecting the concerns of stakeholders in the

decision-making process. This is one of the ways in which public relations builds and protects value.[14]

Lesson – Ask yourself whether you have engaged throughout with all your stakeholders, not just the media

---

Kids Company

This high-profile charity provided support to deprived and vulnerable inner-city children and young people. Its founder and Chief Executive, Camila Batmanghelidjh, was very much the public face of the charity, and it enjoyed widespread support, not least from politicians.

To say the collapse of the charity was controversial would be an understatement. There were allegations of financial mismanagement, a police investigation into allegations of sexual and physical abuse which was launched and subsequently dropped, a government grant which was paid and which the government then attempted to get back, and suggestions that senior politicians, including the then Prime Minister, David Cameron, had ignored advice from officials and had kept funds going to the charity.

Batmanghelidjh throughout continued to protest that she and the charity were being unfairly pursued by the media and politicians. She contended that the charity was in a good financial position and was continuing to deliver for vulnerable young people.

The arguments took place over several months and played out across the media, with no one seemingly willing to back down. The whole episode was a sad reminder that even well-known and well-established charities can become vulnerable to the changing tide of circumstances, not to mention media attention. Whatever the rights or wrongs, a "battle" between leaders and politicians makes for good media coverage. In the case of Kids Company, the Chair of Trustees was also a well-known figure in the media. This brought additional attention.

The loss of such a high-profile charity, and the very public manner of the loss, gave many in the sector pause for reflection.

It demonstrated that no charity can be regarded as "untouchable". Even the profile of its chief executive, its previous good coverage and impeccable political connections did not make Kids Company immune. A "good story" is a "good story" regardless of who is involved. Charities should always be prepared for media interest however unexpected it may be.

Even if an enquiry or story has got the wrong end of the stick or is the result of a baseless grudge, it could be a signal that the leadership has missed something. Communications, rather than just being an external consideration, should also trigger internal review processes.

Leadership teams, including trustees, are required to act in the best interests of the charity to further its purposes. There will always be pressure, not least from donors, to concentrate on beneficiaries and not to "waste" money, whether that be on marketing, communications, or simply good governance and administration. But if these are not right, then everything else can be at risk. That means being prepared to shine a light on all aspects of the charity's operations. As seen from the examples mentioned, many organisations do not address such frailties until forced to do so.

Leadership teams should be confident that they have a supportive environment and culture in place that allows for reviews and critical questioning.

Lesson – A high profile does not offer automatic reputation protection

---

Royal National Lifeboat Institution

It is important also to highlight some of the excellent crisis and reputation management work that charities do. One of the most potentially damaging crises but one which has become a text book example of how to handle a difficult situation was that encountered by the Royal National Lifeboat Institution (RNLI). The problem was identified when graphic sexual imagery combined with the face of a crew member were found printed on mugs at one its lifeboat stations. The national media soon picked up on this and tried to portray the issue of "pornographic mugs" as little more than banter. Accusations of the RNLI being "politically correct" and of over-reacting started to take hold. The spotlight put donations at risk, but the RNLI also had a duty to care for its staff and large numbers of volunteers. For the RNLI, this was a crisis with potentially huge consequences.

I was fortunate enough to discuss the issue with Isla Reynolds, who was a Senior Media Engagement Manager at RNLI and led the external communications team.

I asked her how they first become aware of the problem and whether they immediately appreciated the potential reputational damage:

> The communications team and operations team work closely together on all sorts of things – from responding to major incidents to managing issues. So we have a good relationship and a system in place where issues such as this get flagged pretty early on. In this case, our regional operational manager had briefed their regional communications manager that inappropriate material (mugs with some of the crew's faces superimposed on hardcore pornographic images) had been found at a lifeboat station, and we had prepared reactive lines.
>
> While we knew there was a reputational risk, I don't think we foresaw the angle or the vehemence of some of the reaction from the media or the public. We could just as easily have been criticised for having pornographic material at one of our stations as been censured for standing down volunteers.
>
> The story had been picked up by local media, and we'd hoped that would be it. But we hadn't considered how good this story would be for a tabloid – it was an opportunity to reconstruct a titillating image of a "saucy" mug (no matter if it bore no resemblance to the real thing) and rail against an organisation's perceived heavy-handedness in stepping down the volunteers responsible.

Isla and I spoke about the immediate steps the RNLI took to protect its reputation:

> We issued our reactive lines and worked with our operations team to manage the issue on the ground. It's incredibly important that

PR isn't the only tool used to manage an issue – it has to be combined with action taken to manage/support the people involved, tackle the root cause or address whatever has gone wrong.

The initial lines we had were quite corporate – in cases that involve volunteers or staff, we have to be careful not to betray their legal right to confidentiality. So there's very little we can say without risk of legal ramifications.

Unfortunately, the story did not go away after the first round of local or national coverage. A couple of days into the crisis, the *Daily Mail* rang and wanted a story that linked this issue to other examples of the RNLI responding to poor staff or volunteer behaviour by stepping people down from their roles.

With the situation escalating, we took a new, stronger, more proactive approach. Fundamentally, people needed to know why we'd made these decisions, and a corporate statement wasn't going to cut it.

So we decided to be more transparent – to provide in-depth interviews and give details. I'd started writing a statement (which I was quite pleased with), until one of our regional operations managers – also a lifeboat volunteer for over 20 years, and a good friend, came up to me. He was furious – furious for the organisation, and furious that people thought crew were like they'd seen in the paper. He'd written a video script to get it off his chest, and read it to me. It was way better than my statement and got to the real heart of the matter. No placating people, no apology for our decisions, no backing down. A very different approach. I stole it. And then I and our HR legal counsel presented the risks to our chief executive and chairman – and got their decision within ten minutes.[15]

But it wasn't just the press we were talking to. This new, bold, transparent, detailed response was sent to all our volunteers and staff ahead of the article publishing – we armed them with the information they needed, and trusted them to defend us in their own words. And it was a good thing we did. None of the information from the interviews we did appeared in the article. While this wasn't good, it did give us a platform for a strong response.

We were able to post another statement, publicly online and to our volunteers, that went through the article showing what the *Mail* said, and what we'd said in return.

We spent the weekend responding to comments across social media – something that took three people at any one time as we cycled through the comms team. We also worked with Legal to start writing a complaint to the *Mail* (they wouldn't read it until Monday, so this was not a priority). This later became a letter from the chief executive to be published in the *Mail* (it was).

This approach, and the media attention in general, brought unwelcome focus to the volunteers and staff dealing with a difficult situation. As a charity dependent on public funding, we should absolutely be held up to scrutiny by the press – but there were points during this issue where journalists were knocking on people's relatives' doors or hounding them in the street. So the communications team also provided practical support – we issued guidance on dealing with press harassment and spoke to editors to ask their staff to back off.

After the initial crisis had moved on, I asked Isla what steps the RNLI took to try to repair the initial damage to its reputation.

We actually worked closely with the *Daily Mail*, who initially wanted to do a follow-up piece. We'd already complained to the editor about the first piece (written by a freelancer) and were now working with a staff journalist. Again, we took a transparent approach. I and the regional operations manager met the journalist face-to-face and answered all his questions as transparently as possible. Of course, he was looking for a story and was objective – but he listened to us, appreciated that we were being open, and made the decision not to take the story further based on all the information he had. We now have a good working relationship with this journalist.

To repair the damage done, we took a three-stage approach – respond to initial criticism, demonstrate the RNLI's strengths across all our internal and external channels and media activity (i.e. the incredible lifesaving work of our lifeboat crews and lifeguards), and (after a period of time) slowly feed positive stories into local media about the specific lifeboat station involved. We also developed a series of content used across our internal and external channels that showed there was not a division between staff and volunteers – often using case studies of staff who also volunteered.

This all needed to be supported by efforts by our operations team to support our staff and volunteers at the lifeboat station.

Talking about the key lessons, Isla suggested that:

You must work as one comms team and have a consistent message across internal and external channels, even if the tone is slightly different to suit different audiences.

Think like a tabloid – you can prepare for the worst and get to the heart of the matter in your response, otherwise you risk coming across as quite cold and corporate.

Make sure you're the most trusted source of information – for the public, for your people. And that means trusting people with the detail and then letting them defend you.

Be bold – it's OK to stand by your convictions even if it offends people (as long as you're in the right).

Don't be scared to lose people when you draw lines in the sand, because they are probably the people you don't want anyway. We are pretty clear that having hardcore pornography at a lifeboat station is unacceptable – but not everyone agrees with us. That doesn't mean we should change our principles – but we do need to explain what they are and why they are important to us.

Keep learning – don't do what you have always done and hope it's OK. Keep reviewing what's working well, and do more of it. If it isn't working, change or stop it. This is especially true for messaging – often, a couple of messages really resonate and you can focus on these, refine them and keep using them.

Listen to your front-line people – they're often the best gauge of what really matters and what you need to respond to.

Have a tight and streamlined sign-off process – be prepared to bypass people and ruffle a few feathers if you need to – time is of the essence. Better still, ensure that your leaders trust you and when you need to act without restriction.

Set a high standard – it's the right thing to do to set behaviours and principles and stand by them – it means your people can call out bad behaviour and feel able to do so. Turn a blind eye, and you are implicitly supporting the bad behaviour.

Look on the bright side – it can be an opportunity to talk about topics that we might find hard to talk about. For us, this issue helped us articulate what standard of behaviour we expected and why – and also showed us that the vast majority of our staff and volunteers agreed.

Some audiences reacted differently to others, though:

> Our main learning was that the messages had to be consistent. So our internal audiences needed clear, simple messaging and permission to use these in their own words to answer questions and defend us. And they needed these as early as possible. The media wanted a transparent, non-corporate response. The public wanted us to respect their concerns and answer as transparently as possible (whether or not they agreed with us).

There were particular internal challenges to overcome as well:

> Initially, the challenge was to get a detailed and robust response. But this was because of need to protect individuals' confidentiality. Once the risk to the RNLI's reputation outweighed this, we were able to get a better response agreed very swiftly.
>
> The other internal challenge is reaching all our people. We have staff and volunteers across the UK and Ireland. While staff have easy access to our intranet or email, our volunteers can't or don't access it. So we had to get the messages out on multiple channels, which is hard to do quickly and consistently, and you still can't reach everybody.

The incident took place several years ago, but vigilance is still required:

> The issue does still pop up every now and again, often as an aside during other issues. But we simply respond using the same lines. The things we have changed are our issues response process and our issues planning process, to reflect our learnings. But in a strange way, the crisis actually helped us articulate what we expect from our staff and volunteers – and that they expect from themselves – and this has helped us pre-empt any similar issue.

Issues of importance

Savanta's report *Top 100 Most Loved Charity Brands 2020* suggests that the three ways that charities can inspire love from supporters are:

1) Build a personal connection.
2) Build awareness through communication.
3) Build love through boldness.

The report found that being "caring, trusted and honest" are the expected foundations for a charity. They can drive love from supporters and differentiate their voice in what is a largely crowded sector by being "expert, inspiring and confident".

The more beloved charities enjoy increased support, including financial contributions as well as in-kind support such as word of mouth and social media support.

Being a category "medallist" in the report does not mean that those charities do not face significant challenges. Whilst the Royal Society for the Prevention of Cruelty to Animals (RSPCA) was placed second in the animal welfare category in the report, it has faced complaints about its leadership, the approach taken to prosecutions, and financial issues, amongst others.

We have considered Save the Children's challenges in some detail, but it came second in the report's international aid category. In first place was Comic Relief, famous for Red Nose Day. But it too has not been immune from criticism, including the way it illustrates global poverty and its approach to investment.

The financial affairs of charities have undoubtedly risen in prominence in recent years. It is no longer just about the pay levels of chief executives, but also includes the level of reserves held (Are they too high, and should they instead be spent immediately on beneficiaries?) and investment strategies (are they in line with the ethos of the charity?).

Lesson – Pay attention to what is happening in your sector, because there is no protection in glorious isolation

---

Charity crises frequently come in waves. This is often because charities engage in similar types of activities to one another. Taking the example of fundraising scandals, once one charity was accused of using "chuggers" (charity huggers or muggers, depending on your viewpoint, who raise money for charities on the street using hard-sell methods), then so were a number of others. The use of direct mail to elicit donations came under scrutiny following the death of Olive Cooke, a 92-year-old poppy seller who took her own life. Her death was blamed by the media on charities which "bombarded" her with requests for donations. However, her family did not believe that the requests were to blame for her death.

Both Olive Cooke's case and that of Samuel Rae, who was scammed out of tens of thousands of pounds following his information being sold by charities, led to changes in the rules around fundraising.

In both cases, it was not just one charity that was said to use the methods, but many. Each of them was drawn, in turn, into the crisis. The stories continued for many weeks, and both Olive Cooke's and Samuel Rae's names are etched into the history of UK charities.

No one in these cases had done anything illegal. The practices were, at the time, widely accepted across the sector. However, just because a practice is widespread and legal does not offer much in the way of protection for a reputation when the media and politicians get involved.

Gemma Holding took over as CEO of the Cancer Recovery Foundation in 2015. She immediately uncovered a number of historical concerns with the organisation and its operations that could/would pose a reputational risk to both the charity and herself.

She undertook a number of immediate actions, and as a result of her experience, has a number of recommendations for other leaders:

- *Enlist the support from others who can help you effect change* – In her case, that involved recruiting four new board members to the charity within the first six months, the first new trustees appointed in over a decade. After a lengthy and difficult legal process, the trustees and Holding successfully cut ties with the US-based parent charity and its founder. This enabled a wholesale turnaround across the organisation, including its name, mission, values, services offered and fundraising methods employed.
- *Be brave and act quickly* – Being brave is one of the best pieces of advice Holding would give when dealing with reputational issues. She suggests that it takes courage to make positive decisions when they will likely produce negative outcomes – in her case, this would be a very real loss

of income, in the short term at least, by terminating a long-standing fundraising model. As tempting as it may be to continue with a practice until a suitable replacement is found, this would certainly have taken time. Acting quickly was critical, as within a matter of weeks the charity was featured in a national newspaper front page article about poor charity fundraising practices. At the time of going to press, the foundation was able to respond that it had *already* made changes.

- *Be mindful of the "expert advice" you take* – Taking advice from experts and acting it is something all CEOs have to do. However, Holding believes it is prudent to be discerning with all advice received, even from "experts", to ensure that it sits well with you personally as well as professionally. During her first few months as the CEO of the Cancer Recovery Foundation, she queried a number of the financial and accounting practices and was assured that they were all legal and complied with the charity Statement of Recommended Practice. But, as she was keen to stress, in the charity sector especially, just because you *can* do something, it certainly doesn't mean that you *should*. It is absolutely essential to act with integrity and not do anything you are uncomfortable with, even if you have been advised to do so.

The turnaround Gemma and her team achieved has extended across the whole organisation, and has not been limited to just one area or project. She has learnt that acting with integrity is not always easy, and was acutely aware that negative results could stem from positive decisions, but felt that ultimately these were right in the long term for the charity and its reputation.

The renamed Cancer Support UK has learnt the importance of striving to "do better" even if the consequences are not immediately recognised. Gemma's example demonstrates that wholescale positive turnaround is possible, although it is certainly not easy. For Gemma, "it is up to all of us to protect the reputation of the sector, and champion best practice".

The issues continue

Too many organisations, not just charities, fail to appreciate that just because a behaviour is accepted practice does not make it right.

Organisations need to ensure they are making their own decisions rather than simply doing the same as others and believing that it offers protection.

A useful approach is to consider the reports issued following crises at other organisations and employ them as a baseline for your own actions and activity. They offer an opportunity to learn from the mistakes of others. Since Oxfam's internal review recommended the appointment of a Chief Ethics Officer and a confidential reporting system for staff to raise concerns, then why not consider introducing something similar for your own organisation?

The reality is that confidential reporting systems are nothing new in the corporate sector, but may instead be called "whistle-blower hotlines". Best practice should be learned from wherever it exists. This approach might not have solved all the issues faced by – in this case – Oxfam, but it might have helped identify and deal with them earlier.

Some organisations adopt the tactic of broadening the "blame" to others. In that way, everyone potentially suffers from the reputational damage. In a competitive sense, this may have some logic. However, if everyone does badly, then ultimately the groups they are trying to protect, the beneficiaries of the charities, are harmed. The New Philanthropy Capital (NPC) *State of the Sector 2020* report found widespread agreement amongst charity leaders that public trust in the sector had fallen. The Edelman Trust *Barometer 2020* also identified continued issues of trust for charities (NGOs, as Edelman specifies them), but at least in this report they are seen as behaving ethically (against business, media and government).

As highlighted, the reputations of charities and the sector itself have been declining in recent years. According to an interview with Vicky Browning, Chief Executive of the Association of Chief Executives of Voluntary Organisations, "The public – fairly so – has a high expectation of how charities will respond." On the Oxfam scandal, she went onto say:

> The challenge it had was with the sense of reputation. The desire to protect reputation is understandable because reputation is important for charities and we want people to trust us. However,

we cannot protect our reputation at the expense of protecting the people and causes that we are here to serve.[16]

This was a theme echoed by James White:

I would suggest that falsely denying accusations, or even trying to muddy the water, is unlikely to work for a charity concerned with a long-term future! Longer-term, it's important to learn the lessons. It's not always easy to accept that your own processes might be inadequate, so asking an impartial body to help you with this evaluation might be sensible.

The National Society for the Prevention of Cruelty to Children

The example of the National Society for the Prevention of Cruelty to Children (NSPCC) demonstrates that decisions need to be considered carefully from the outset rather than simple knee-jerk reactions being made.

To great fanfare, the charity announced transgender activist Munroe Bergdorf as Childline's first LGBT+ campaigner. Bergdorf, a model, has long been a high-profile campaigner, but had not been without controversy prior to her appointment – for instance, having been sacked by L'Oréal for a Facebook post (which she later deleted).

Following the announcement, the charity was hit by hostility on social media accusing Bergdorf of not being the right sort of role model for children, criticising her offer for children to get in touch with her on social media, and of being a "porn model", amongst other comments.

The charity swiftly released a statement saying that Bergdorf would have "no ongoing relationship with Childline or the NSPCC" and was not an ambassador for the charity.

It also stated that: "The NSPCC does not support, endorse or authorise any personal statements made by any celebrities who contribute to campaigns. Childline is available to all children without condition to provide support whatever the nature of their concerns".

This in turn brought a wave of fury from both staff, who wrote an open letter condemning the move, and the LGBT+ community. This was not least because the charity had failed to speak to Bergdorf before making the announcement.

Bergdorf complained that the NSPCC had given into transphobia, and urged supporters to make donations to a charity that supports transgender and gender diverse children and their parents. That charity, Mermaids, saw an increase in donations of around 300%, whilst the NSPCC saw just under 200 cancelled donations, though Bergdorf urged people not to make such cancellations.

As a result of the second wave of backlash, the charity's chief executive, Peter Wanless, had to issue not just an apology to Bergdorf, but also a lengthy statement detailing what went wrong and what would be done differently next time. It demonstrated that the charity realised that it had initially misread comments on Twitter as representing wider public feeling and, as a consequence, alienated the very community it was setting out to support. It had to do something pretty drastic if it was to have any chance of ensuring that the feeling left at the end, about not being there for LGBT+ children, was really the exact opposite.

The charity adopted an approach that questioned its own decision-making procedures and completely exonerated Munroe Bergdorf. It did not stand by its own process, and instead chose to admit they had got it wrong.

A tendency to over-react is something that can happen when organisations think about their reputation, according to James White:

> On occasion, organisations inadvertently make situations worse by feeling an urge to respond to every perceived criticism.
>
> Equally, there can be inaction! Sometimes organisations fail to recognise the severity of a situation, meaning that critical voices will fill the space left unfilled by the organisation in the firing line.

Reflecting on these and others issues that charities have faced in recent years, Chloe Stables, a leading charity communications expert, suggested that charities often fail because of their "lack of pace". She suggests that:

in comparison to the fast-moving 24-hour news cycle, the charity governance world can seem positively glacial. Some organisations have struggled with the pace of internal processes (such as complicated senior management or board structures). The window of opportunity for getting ahead of a story and shaping the narrative can be incredibly small.

Her advice is that "it's worth thinking through even very simple things like how your press office might contact the chair of trustees on a Sunday to get appropriate sign-off and make sure all the decision-makers are in the loop".

She also believes that:

often, organisations will focus on what they need to say to a journalist or how they need to respond to a breaking story. It can be hard, obviously, when the spotlight falls on an organisation, but the most important thing is to take a step back – analyse the situation and respond appropriately – often, this will mean taking practical steps to solve the problem, but also taking appropriate advice and guidance on what options are open to you.

Moving on to the practical steps that charities should take to help build and maintain a reputation, she pointed to the necessity for action in three areas:

1) *Transparency* – "In general, people are not looking for perfection: they're not looking to audit you, they just want to know you care. Having the figures available shows you understand they're concerned about what you do with their money. The numbers themselves, within reason, don't really matter, it's the fact that they're there that matters. There's also something really important here about how and where you present this type of information. If it's buried in a complicated table on page 64 of your annual review and accounts that probably doesn't feel very transparent to most people. Most charities now have a very straightforward page on their websites that it's easy to signpost people too".

2) *Lose the gloss/adopt a more human approach* – "It's much more believable if you're open and honest about the things that have gone right and the things that have gone wrong. The Clic Sargent impact report was (quite rightly in my view) held up as a really good and useful model for talking about failure and what we can learn from it".[17]

3) *Show, don't tell* – "The best response is often one which isn't about saying something, but actually making change happen. The fundraising scandals boiled down to what in some respects is an ethical dilemma: how hard should you press a potential donor in order to raise money for a good cause? The reality is that what charities were doing was not in step with what the public, quite reasonably, expected of them. And no amount of even the best communications can be a sticking plaster for a fundamental problem within a charity or charities. The response from the sector and government was swift, setting up a review of fundraising practice which recommended a number of key changes to the way charities fundraise and the way these practices are regulated".

In terms of preparation, Chloe suggests that charities should:

1) *Think ahead* – "Trustees and others should build in a regular reflection on what are the most likely things that could impact on your reputation. Think about how you might deal with a potentially negative scenario and what are the steps you can take to help mitigate this. Many organisations use a risk register to help with this process".

2) *Think practically* – "If something did go wrong, who would need to be involved in making decisions about the response, how would you contact them, who would lead on certain aspects?"

3) *Think about all your stakeholders* – "When things go wrong, it's really easy to focus on those that might be the most vocal, such as MPs or others likely to comment on a story, so it's important to consider all your stakeholders and prioritise accordingly – from those affected directly, to your staff and volunteers, through to funders".

> *Lesson – Always allow space for reflection*

Final thoughts

To many, it appears that the standards charities are expected to attain are higher than for others. But just as charities were late to experience the pressures of reputation management, the standards they are now held to should be an example to others.

However, adopting a more robust response to crises will not be without its challenges. Just take the Oxfam example. Any current stand also means having a good knowledge about the history of an organisation and decisions made before current leadership teams may have been involved. The Save the Children example shows that you need to be completely on top of all previous decisions in any current response.

This is another reason for immediately confronting challenges and being seen to deal with them forcefully. Otherwise, problems are simply being stored up for future leaders. In a selfish way, some may not care, but that is not putting the best interests of the organisation or its beneficiaries first.

More than ever, charities need to pay attention to what is going on around them. They need to have a good idea of where the next line of attack may come from, and that means having good monitoring systems in place. James White believes that: "If the media are lasering in on a charity in a similar position (in terms of beneficiaries supported by that charity, or income source) then it would be wise to assume that you might be next!"

You will only understand this if you know what is going on.

Notes

1 Institute of Fundraising, PwC, Charity Finance Group (2014).
2 Charity Commission for England and Wales (July 2018).
3 De la Fuente Sabate and de Quevedo Puento (2003).
4 Charity Commission for England and Wales (May 2018).
5 Ibid.

6 Younger (2013) (www.gov.uk/government/speeches/protecting-your-charitys-reputation).

7 Charity Commission for England and Wales (2016).

8 Swinford and Ward (2018).

9 BBC (2018).

10 Jack (2019).

11 *The Times* (2021).

12 Grafton-Green (2018) (www.standard.co.uk/news/world/oxfam-admits-rehiring-sacked-aid-worker-as-desmond-tutu-quits-ambassador-role-a3767766.html).

13 Charity Commission for England and Wales (2019).

14 CIPR (2019).

15 You can read the statement at RNLI (2018) (https://rnli.org/news-and-media/2018/may/12/rnli-response-to-todays-article-in-the-daily-mail).

16 Ker (2018).

17 The details can be seen at Clic Sargent (2019) (www.clicsargent.org.uk/clic-sargent-publishes-its-annual-impact-and-accountability-report-the-good-the-bad-and-the-ugly/) and an overview at Third Sector (2019) (www.thirdsector.co.uk/clic-sargents-impact-report-difficult-second-album/management/article/1664106).

References

Andrew Jack, 'How Save the Children's UK chief executive is rebuilding trust among staff', *Financial Times*, 1 September 2019.

BBC, 'Save the Children review details harassment of staff', 8 October 2018.

Charity Commission for England and Wales, 'Case note, Age UK', 19 April 2016.

Charity Commission for England and Wales, 'The essential trustee: What you need you know, what you need to do', May 2018.

Charity Commission for England and Wales, 'Trust in charities, 2018', July 2018.

Charity Commission for England and Wales, 'Inquiry report: Summary findings and conclusions Oxfam', 11 June 2019.

CIPR, 'Oxfam's approach to reputation management "exposed the charity to undue risk"', 12 June 2019.

Clic Sargent, 'Clic Sargent publishes its annual impact and accountability report – The good, the bad and the ugly', Press Release, Clic Sargent, 29 October 2019.

Edelman Trust Barometer, 'Trust: Competence And Ethics', *Edelman*, 19 January 2020 (https://www.edelman.com/trust/2020-trust-barometer).

Henry Ker, 'UK: Vicky Browning: Charity governance after Oxfam', *Mondaq Business Briefing*, 11 April 2018.

Institute of Fundraising, PwC, Charity Finance Group, 'Managing in a new normal', April 2014.

J. M. de la Fuente Sabate and E. de Quevedo Puento, 'Empirical analysis of the relationship between corporate reputation and financial performance', *Corporate Reputation Review*, 6(2), 2003, pp. 161–177.

nfpSynergy, *Trust in Charities (Year 2017)*, 23 January 2018.

NPC, 'State of the sector 2020', 18 May 2020 (https://www.thinknpc.org/resource-hub/stots2020/).

Patrick Grafton-Green, 'Oxfam admits re-hiring sacked aid worker as Desmond Tutu quits ambassador role', *Evening Standard*, 15 February 2018.

RNLI, 'RNLI response to today's article in the Daily Mail', Press Release, 12 May 2018.

Sam Younger, 'Protecting your charity's reputation', *Speech*, 13 July 2013.

Savanta, 'Top 100 most loved charity brands 2020', 20 February 2020.

Steven Swinford and Victoria Ward, 'Save the Children boss in text scandal', *The Daily Telegraph*, 21 February 2018.

The Times, 'The *Times* view on the Oxfam scandal: Enough is enough', *The Times*, 2 April 2021.

Third Sector, 'Clic Sargent's impact report: The difficult second album', *Third Sector*, 30 October 2019.

5

POLITICS

BEST FRIEND OR WORST ENEMY?

The role that politics plays is critical in reputation management. Legislatures, elected members, ministers, prime ministers and presidents – all the parts that make up the governments of countries have real power. They can pass new laws, introduce new regulations, establish regulators, create taxes, or impose fines and prison for poor behaviour. Failing to manage political audiences is unforgiveable because of the potential consequences. Even if a politician simply makes an adverse comment or issues a hostile tweet, that can inflict reputational damage.

On the other hand, good political relations will mean less danger of intervention from policy-makers and regulators.

This chapter considers ways in which organisations can manage their reputations when dealing with political audiences. It should not be ignored that they too have their own reputations to protect, and that is often why they choose to intervene. If they are not seen to pronounce on major issues or take action, what could the consequences be for them?

DOI: 10.4324/9781003293880-6

Do not forget that politicians are unlike any other audience leaders have to deal with. Why? They have to stand up and put themselves forward for election. They expose themselves to the public at regular intervals and ask for their votes. In the US, of course, many other public officials also have to be elected into office, and that puts them under the same types of public pressure.

> Lesson – Politicians can inflict real reputational and organisational damage

Politicians

The need for a good understanding of what is taking place should be the foundation of political engagement. Monitoring government statements, what discussions are taking place in parliaments and assemblies, and the questions being asked start to deliver the political intelligence required to make decisions about engagement.

Organisations that are beset by struggles, often in the courts; conflict between companies; a failure to deal with issues of public concern; regular adverse media and social media attention – all these attract political attention and, as a consequence, likely intervention.

A key aspect of reputation management when dealing with any audience, but especially politicians, is that you have to tell them your side of any story. You need to increase their level of awareness about you and your issues. Certainly, having the support of others is useful, but the first step should be getting your briefings right.

My approach to political engagement is that it should be pro-active. Opportunities do not often just land at your feet. Instead, you need to undertake outreach, develop the networks and have a well-developed argument.

Briefings, at least initially, are often in a written format. There is standard advice about the content and length of a briefing paper – around two sides of A4 – but there should a little more to it than that:

- Do not just rely on the power of a narrative – however eloquent you may be, a stream of words saying "this works", "that does not", "we need", etc. may be interesting, but will do little to convince anyone.

- Do present the evidence – any good briefing paper has to have some evidence, either case studies or data. Without it, a briefing paper can read just like a political wish list. The key messages in the document should be related directly to this evidence.
- Do provide infographics – within the general confines of keeping briefing papers brief, do think about making papers look and feel a little more enticing. Consider whether the evidence can be presented in an interesting way. This can be particularly useful when it comes to turning briefing papers into blogs, newsletters and other communications materials to assist engagement with other external audiences.
- Do be prepared to test the briefing paper by sharing it before it is formally issued – a good briefing paper will be seen by a range of audiences, so it needs to be understood by experts and non-experts. It is useful to get a range of people to read and provide feedback on it.
- Do be able to answer the questions – when the experts and non-experts come back with questions, these will doubtless be similar to the ones that politicians and civil servants/officials will ask. Before launching your briefing paper on an unsuspecting audience, make sure you can answer these questions. A failure to be able to do so will undermine your case.
- Do avoid jargon – many of those who see the paper could well fail to understand an argument if it is full of jargon: it normally only confuses rather than clarifies. The idea is not to speak in a special code that only expert audiences can understand.
- Do not go on for too long – politicians are easily bored, especially with too much detail at the outset. Keep focused on the essentials to grab their attention. The detail can come later.
- Do have supporting materials available – if the briefing paper is not enough, then have some wider papers available and think about what else the audience may find useful. Could that be related to meeting with key team members or those involved in any case studies cited? Maybe a site visit would be illustrative for them?
- Do always think about the follow-up – a lot of the art in a good briefing paper comes from fully understanding the intended audience, its timescales, expectations and the processes under which it has to operate. It looks outwards rather than inwards. A good briefing paper should be considered a taster.

- Do always offer a solution – if there is one point to remember, then it is this: always explain to the audience how the issue can be dealt with. Be able to explain what the policy ask is that would solve the problem.

Getting the briefings right enables an organisation to start to build relationships of trust with politicians. It is important to appreciate from the outset that, just as with any other relationship, time and effort need to be invested. You need to think ahead and recognise the benefits a trusted relationship will bring.

The simple fact is that politicians do need assistance when it comes to policy development, but the task is to help them appreciate that. You have to demonstrate that your expertise and insight are invaluable to them and, in essence, will help them to do their jobs better, avoid mistakes and deliver better policies.

So how can trust be built with politicians and policy-makers?

- Be pro-active – do not wait to be asked to get involved, instead show initiative where it comes to engagement. Seek out opportunities. These could range from debates in parliament through to committee inquiries or policy consultations.
- Deliver what you promise – when engagement has taken place, then make sure you deliver; make good on the promises made. A period of silence and/or non-delivery endangers the relationship even if it is a more established one.
- Think about their needs and priorities, not just your own – if it looks like you are being self-centred and are only building the relationship for your own ends, then the relationship is put at risk. Such a transactional exchange is not a relationship, and will have no long-term future. You need to think about the pressures on them – timescales, who may be making demands on them, what they need to deliver etc.
- Bear in mind your wider reputation – politicians and policy-makers will consider your general reputation. A poor reputation makes relationships more difficult to establish in the first instance. Over the longer term, a dip in reputation can mean that friends become more

elusive and are less likely to listen to you. That is especially the case if the reputational challenge goes to the heart of your capability/ what you actually do. The ramifications of such damage will ripple throughout a network.

- Keep focused on what makes them tick – this is especially important when thinking about political engagement, as elected representatives will appreciate contact in areas of policy interest to them, related to constituency matters etc. However, being too party political, not thinking about the wider political setting, or forgetting that there are such things as elections will risk relationships.

Ideally, companies need to develop a capability to work with governments and political audiences. Often, this does not happen because the potential impact of government is underestimated or leaders assume they can deal with politicians.

Lesson – There are no short cuts to building political trust

Inquiries

Invariably if something goes wrong, the political spotlight arrives, often in the form of a parliamentary or congressional inquiry.

In the UK Parliament, these are usually undertaken by Select Committees. These are small groups of Members of Parliament, or members of the House of Lords, that investigate a specific issue or scrutinise the work of a government department to hold it to account. The committees hold inquiries to which written evidence can be submitted and have the power to call witnesses to appear before them. Committees will publish reports at the end of their inquiries, which will include recommendations for action, and the government has to respond to them. All political systems have similar committees, such as Senate Committees in the US. Whilst the specific powers vary, the gravity with which they should be treated does not. Fail to take them seriously at your peril – not least because of the impact on reputations.

Inquiries are often led by the news agenda, so when a big issue hits the headlines, then a committee will invariably announce an inquiry. The political audiences need to be seen to be taking the issue seriously and doing all they can to deal with it. Fundamentally, they know that they cannot always deliver change themselves. But what they can do is exert influence through their ability to impact on an organisation's reputation, and they can perform a similar role with their own domestic government as well. That ability to wield power over a reputation is really the biggest weapon they have.

Some have refused to appear before Select Committees in the UK. These include Mark Zuckerberg, Mike Ashley (Sports Direct) and Dominic Cummings, the former head of Vote Leave who subsequently went on to be chief adviser to Prime Minister Boris Johnson. The committees all made darkly threatening noises about the implications, but none of the individuals ended up in the Tower of London as a result of their refusal to appear. Instead, the committees turned their attention to reputation shaming.

The implications for those concerned can therefore still be enormous.

If we consider how an organisation should contend with being on the receiving end of a committee inquiry, then it is possible to put a strategy in place:

1) *The crisis* – If you are in the eye of a significant crisis, then the best assumption is that an inquiry will come your way. As already highlighted, make political audiences part of the group you brief on the issue – highlight the context, your actions and the future.

2) *The announcement* – When the inevitable does happen and the inquiry is announced, then that will bring with it another round of unwanted media coverage. The chair of the committee will be given plenty of space to air their views on the issue, say why the inquiry is being held and what they hope to achieve. You may be able to submit a comment by way of response, but the coverage will be very largely negative.

3) *The submissions* – In the case of UK Select Committees, such papers are made public, so everything has to be considered in that light. It does, though, provide an opportunity to state your position, what

went wrong, what changes are being made and what the future will look like. A well-crafted paper can take the initial sting out of an inquiry, but equally it may enrage. Tone and approach are critical. Some organisations have chosen to use such submissions as part of a media campaign as well – often as part of a fight-back. Again, this is not without its risks, as committees can believe that such a strategy is too combative and possibly not deferential enough to them.

4) *The oral sessions* – This is where the real damage can be inflicted. Not all committee hearings adopt an adversarial approach. Many are there to get to the bottom of issues, discuss policy options or hold government to account. But in the circumstances we are most concerned with, those giving the evidence are often on the defensive. They are there to explain to the political audiences what has gone wrong, what they got wrong and what they are going to do about it. The committee is there is make a splash and ensure that an example is made of those giving evidence. Added to what went wrong, they can also be looking at who is going to take the blame for the failure.

This approach can infect the nature of the hearing. Politicians can have a tendency to grandstand under such circumstances. Their questions may be designed not to elicit information, but to secure a response that makes those giving evidence look ill-prepared, deficient in running their organisation or simply to get them to say something embarrassing. Why? The hearings are public, they may be broadcast live, and the best bits, the grandstanding parts, may be used in news broadcasts and social media clips. For the really big organisations, the global companies, comments can be carried on news outlets the world over. Mark Zuckerberg's appearance before the US Senate's Commerce and Judiciary Committees in April 2018 to discuss data privacy and Russian disinformation was an example of such global interest.

5) *The outcome* – Whatever the committee or hearing, there will be some form of outcome: a report, policy recommendations etc. Governments themselves are rarely compelled to implement the recommendations, but they can be adopted, especially if they are

seen to offer an effective solution to the problem. The announcement of the outcome can be another opportunity for reputational
damage – the issue is summarised, the appearances replayed and
the chair of the committee or inquiry gets a chance to front the
coverage.

From start to finish, a politically led committee hearing or an inquiry
needs to be carefully prepared for.

> *Lesson – Monitor developments so that you do not get caught out unexpectedly*

The reality is that such committees demand deference. They have to be
taken seriously, and at all stages in engagement with them, deference
must be shown. This does not mean that an organisation has to take everything lying down. Committees will always try to stretch their powers
a little or imply that they can make demands with which you have no
choice but to comply. That may not be the case. Knowing their powers,
and their limits, is always useful. The decision may be to turn down certain requests they make. That is not without its risks, not least in terms
of reputation, but it could be right thing to do.

When appearing before a committee or hearing, it is essential to undertake sufficient preparation. The senior leaders need to practise, practise,
practise. This means taking into account everything from knowing the
types of questions that will come their way through to the personali-
ties of those asking the question. A full immersive rehearsal experience
means that they can perform to their maximum potential on the day.

Of course, leaders have different ways of preparing, but absolutely no
one should ever go into a session without having been prepared first.

In terms of questions, there are always ones about "the basis" of the
problem itself, but again with reputation in mind, there are often questions posed that on the face of it have little to do with the issue at hand.
Instead, they seem deliberately designed to embarrass and play well in
the media or to be used as a clip on social media. Who can forget the

Google executive who was unable to say how much he earned, despite the session being about the amount of tax Google pays in the UK? These "curveball" or "left-field" questions need to be thought about as well. They could end up being the most unfair, and also the most damaging.

It is often the failure to fully comprehend the nature of the deference required that can derail a session, increase the tension and annoy politicians. However experienced a leader may be, there is no substitute (at least in the eyes of politicians) for standing for election. It means that they have a mandate others simply do not have. With that mandate comes a set of expectations that they will look after their constituents and the needs of the country as a whole. Leaders of an organisation, on the other hand, "just" need to look after it and its stakeholders. If they fail to do that, they can be removed. Leaders may be answerable to boards, investors, trustees and others, but these are relatively small groups when compared to the numbers politicians are answerable to. Even the smallest electoral constituency in the UK has a population of over 60,000, and in the US the smallest district has a population of around 500,000.

It is quite easy to be cynical about politicians, but the weight of expectation and external pressure on them is quite enormous. Of course, as in all walks of life, some are better and more effective in their role than others. Some take the role more seriously than others. But they know that ultimately, the electorate will decide their fate and that the only way to continue in office is to deliver for the electorate.

Taking the time to understand the motivation of politicians and government helps in devising appropriate responses.

Coming back to the challenge of dealing with committees, the approach should be to:

- Answer the questions.
- Don't answer back.
- Don't ask your own questions.
- Be as constructive as possible.
- Avoid looking bored or getting distracted.
- Never lose your temper!

If you fail to understand the importance of deference, then that can derail the whole appearance.

Lesson – Preparation is the key

Some leaders feel the need to consider reams of information and every possible angle a hearing could take. This is an approach that works for some, but the reality is that many questions are really just variations on the same theme. Having ring binders full of information and possible responses is certainly taking the session seriously, but can have the unfortunate side effect of demonstrating, to some, that the person is not really on top of the issues. If the ring binder is constantly referred to during the session itself, then the politicians can get frustrated by the delays. Instead of an honest approach, the session will feel overly pre-prepared. That is not the sort of interaction the politicians will be seeking.

There will be some repetition on the part of those appearing before a hearing. The key is to answer each question as if it is the first time it has been asked.

Another challenge to demonstrating appropriate deference is being asked questions by those who clearly do not fully understand the issues and still keeping the answers civil. Hearings often deal with complex technical matters, but not all the politicians asking the questions will really understand them. That can lead to frustrations, but these should never seep out into the responses. If time needs to be taken to explain, perhaps not for the first time, what the position is, then that is what should be done.

Some leaders prefer to hone their approach and be less reliant on the ring binder, the information bible from which they should not stray. The approach taken by Mark Zuckerberg in his appearances before the Senate Commerce and Judiciary Committees shows that something much shorter and sharper can be more effective.[1]

Given the pressure of a hearing, there is not the time to navigate large documents when under intense questioning. Such pauses play badly, and often secure a sarcastic follow-up. This, in reputational terms, is counterproductive.

Not all questions asked during a committee session are well considered. As well as not always understanding the issues, politicians may simply have been handed the questions to ask. That is what makes some politicians particularly effective, as they clearly do understand the issue at hand. This shows itself in the quality of the follow-up questions. A politician who doesn't "get it" is ill-equipped to ask meaningful follow-ups.

There are many tactics questioners can adopt, from a soft starting question to playing "good cop, bad cop" with colleagues, or using a tag team approach to maintain the pressure on an issue over a long period of time.

The more one knows and understands what can happen, the better and more effective the preparation can be.

Whilst all the pressure may be the in room itself, it is impossible to ignore the wider circus that comes with a hearing as well. Particularly in the US, the media will often carry testimony live. This is big box office, depending on who is giving evidence and who the politicians involved are. But part of what makes some political approaches so effective is that they work brilliantly on social media as well.

These channels can amplify the damage if a slip is made or a telling question left answered. The sad reality, though, is that if the session goes well for those being questioned, there is not always the same level of interest. Tactics and the approach on the day could be designed to try to secure that wider coverage, for instance by giving the media a memorable quote to carry which improves a position. If that fails to work, then a social media campaign to convey the "best bits" of a session from the witness's perspective may be an option. It is extremely unlikely to go viral, but it does ensure that your side of the story can be found more easily.

Lesson – Politicians can easily amplify their messages, inflicting yet more damage

---

There may also be a range of audiences only too willing to pass comment on any hearings and put themselves forward to provide media comments. This can be a competitive space, so it should never be assumed that your position, as you see it, will be adequately reflected in the coverage. Always be prepared to make every effort to get your side across, even if things have gone well, but particularly if proceedings have not gone as hoped. In those circumstances, there could be some drastic action to take, but never believe that it is all over.

Committees will hold inquiries and hearings into issues directly related to you, meaning there will be evidence sessions with opponents, competitors, campaigning groups and others who potentially do not have your best interests at heart.

It is always best to consider the types of preparatory activity that can be put in place. You could consider briefings to friends and allies to see if they may be prepared to stand up for you on the day as well. There is certainly no rule that you should leave what committee members say on the day unchallenged. Indeed, if it is left unchallenged, then that will be seen by some as an admittance of guilt.

For more challenging issues, committees will look to hear from the victims or those who have suffered most. This helps them build a case against the perpetrators, who will often appear at a later date. For instance, the Culture, Media and Sport Select Committee, as part of its inquiry into "immersive and addictive technologies", took evidence from gamers who had had real financial problems as a result of playing video games.

In the case of Oxfam, written evidence from a safeguarding expert, William Anderson, provided everything an eager media would have hoped for. The comments were exactly the type that force governments and regulators to take action:

> Rather than focusing on the intrinsic risks that aid crises pose to the vulnerable, Oxfam's overriding concerns were twofold. First, expanding their services or "Brand Penetration", as I heard it referred to (there were even discussions about "increasing market share") and secondly, "reputational risk".[2]

If you are looking for an example of how not to conduct yourself, then take a look at then Chief Executive of TSB Paul Pester dealing with the Treasury Select Committee,[3] explaining the failure of TSB's services and IT system. As the Guardian said at the time: "Any ambitious junior bank executives out there should watch that hearing again closely, as an example of how not to handle a select committee".[4]

Some hearings are deliberately set up for the pure theatre. The Treasury Select Committee's hearings into the banking crisis after 2008 put former bank chief executives together on the same panel. Each apologised, one after the other, for not having done more to prevent the banking collapse.

In many ways, the banking sector has yet to recover its reputation from the time of the collapse. It was not as if the sector was a shining light in the first place, and the challenges continue to add up – misselling products, branch closures and IT failings, to name but a few. When it comes, more recently, to the COVID-19 support mechanisms, then the banks in the UK have again been under pressure over their administration of business support schemes. The threat of new government regulation remains very real for the sector, and any missteps may cost them dear.

Iain Anderson, co-founder and Executive Chairman of Cicero/AMO, agreed, suggesting that:

> A select committee appearance can make or break a brand or an individual. Getting the tone right is key but also being on top of all the questions you might get asked. Preparation and empathy are key. Sort your problem before you appear or come armed with a public policy recommendation that MPs can get their teeth into.

Amongst a range of poorly handled sessions, he pointed to three examples:

- Matt Barrett – when the former Barclays CEO appeared in front of the Treasury Select Committee, he said that he would not let his daughter use a Visa card given the high interest rate. He had to leave the bank shortly afterwards as his reputation was so badly affected.
- Rupert Murdoch – appearing in front of the Culture, Media and Sport Select Committee on the phone hacking that went on at some titles owned by his News International, Murdoch said "this is the most humble day of my life", but sadly, no one believed him.

- Sir Philip Green – appearing in front of the Work and Pensions Select Committee talking about the British Home Stores pension scheme, he showed his disdain for the process by snapping at MPs, "Do you mind not looking at me like that? It's really disturbing".

On a much more positive note, Iain was keen to point to:

- AXA CEO Paul Evans appearing in front of the Transport Select Committee, saying that his company would take a leadership position and ban referral fees for ambulance-chasing lawyers.
- Blackstone MD David Blitzer appearing in front of the Treasury Select Committee on the inquiry into private equity, showing the long-term nature of his firm's investments and then becoming part of a government commission. This followed a media firestorm when one fund manager had said that they paid less tax than their cleaner.

Iana Vidal, a leading public affairs practitioner, stressed the need to send the right level of people to give evidence. In other words, seniority counts. If a committee believes that it is not going to speak to someone at the very top of an organisation, then that can sour relations from the very outset. Iana highlighted the Culture, Media and Sport Committee inquiry into misinformation during COVID-19, which involved representatives from Google, Twitter and Facebook:

> I think that was always destined to be a tough show because those companies failed to send senior representatives, but it looks like they all failed to satisfy the committee's questions, so are now being hauled in to go through the whole thing again – a less than ideal result.

This is a critical consideration when it comes to any period in the political spotlight. They are rarely one-off events. Instead, once the spotlight comes, it tends to remain.

Lesson – Never underestimate the theatre of hearings and the reputational dangers they can bring

---

COVID-19 will doubtless prove to be a "good" example of this. There will continue to be inquiries into who did what and when. Much of this will involve companies as well.

British Airways has already been on the receiving end of one of the most critical Select Committee reports of recent years. On releasing a report on the impact of the coronavirus pandemic on the aviation sector, the Chair of the Transport Committee, Huw Merriman MP, said:

> The impact of coronavirus may sadly mean that the loss of some jobs in the aviation sector is justified. The behaviour of British Airways and its parent company, IAG, is not. It falls well below the standards expected from any employer, especially in light of the scale of taxpayer subsidy, at this time of national crisis. It is unacceptable that a company would seek to drive this level of change under the cover of a pandemic.
> This wanton destruction of a loyal work force cannot appear to go without sanction – by Government, parliamentarians or paying passengers who may choose differently in future. We view it as a national disgrace.[5]

It was this last comment that received the widest coverage, and whilst the company disputed the committee's conclusions, there is little disputing the reputational damage inflicted. At the very least, British Airways has ground to make up with government and politicians.

Political mistakes

Getting to the heady heights of leadership in an organisation does not instantly bring with it the ability to deal with government, politics or politicians. The trouble is that many like to think it does, and that can lead to problems.

They may not talk to the specialist teams that are available to them in-house or as consultants, and often prefer to head off on their own path to do what feels instinctively right to them.

Here are five of the most common mistakes leaders make when dealing with political stakeholders:

- *A lack of listening skills* – With the best will in the world, politicians like to talk and they have opinions, so it is important to be prepared to consider and listen to them properly. There will be a natural temptation to put your side across very forcefully, but the more you take that approach, the less likely it is to be effective. The critical thing to remember, as previously mentioned, is that politicians are very different – they put themselves up for election, whereas organisational leaders do not. This means that their motivations and requirements are different from yours. They may coincide, but that may only happen for a very fleeting moment. The key is to capture that moment.
- *A lack of training* – Training is often on offer, but a level of self-confidence can often bring an assumption that suggests it is not needed. A swift reference to some of the inquiries discussed in this chapter and the follow-up media coverage should be enough to change minds. Media training will be taken, so why not political engagement training?
- *An obsession with "the top"* – The people at the very senior levels of government are not always the ones you need to engage with. An angry letter fired off to a prime minister or president in haste may make a leader feel better, but it is highly unlikely to be effective. In some circumstances, starting at the top can add delays that could hinder dealing with the issue, and in the worst-case scenario, could even be counterproductive.
- *A failure to appreciate previous contact and positions* – Not every meeting starts with a blank sheet of paper: most organisations have a history with an individual, political party or policy issue. Without the full facts and knowledge of each of these, mistakes can be made. The leader needs to know the issues from all angles and the questions that are likely to come at them. There is the chance that they may not be the right person to handle the meeting. But with early internal discussions, these issues can all be resolved and agreed. When this isn't the case, the unexpected and nasty surprise may not come until the meeting itself, and by that time the damage may already have been done.
- *A lack of contrition* – Quite simply, the leader is not the most important person in the room. That can come as a bit of a shock to some, and

the ability to show a degree of deference is appreciated by many politicians. Depending on the circumstances of the engagement, there may also need to be some level of openness or apology. Again, this can come back to good preparation. If politicians believe that you are being obtuse or failing to be open with them about problems, then relations can quickly sour. A series of key messages might work in short media interviews, but they do not work in more detailed political engagement.

Much of this is really focused on good communications, the willingness to seek out and listen to the advice that is available and knowing the needs of the audience.

Lesson – Never underestimate the importance of deference in a political relationship

---

Politics and government are considered by executives as areas they can deal with on their own. The reality is that real and lasting damage can be done. Reputations can be put on the line.

Politicians, at all levels, do have power, and they come with a set of expectations.

Poor actions and engagement can actually increase the level of scrutiny. Leaders should remember that before simply engaging with politicians.

Politicians themselves do not want to suffer from guilt by association. What votes are they likely to gain for standing beside any organisation or individual with a poor reputation?

There is also political capital to be made from politicians being seen to deal strongly and effectively with those who have a poor reputation. Strong politicians taking action wins votes!

The forms of intervention can vary from direct attacks in the media through to regulatory measures, and committee hearings and inquiries of the types highlighted.

Mark Zuckerberg provided testimony to the House of Representatives Committee on Financial Services primarily focused on Facebook's plans for the Libra, its own cryptocurrency. What was most interesting in the session was Zuckerberg's comment: "I understand we're not the ideal messenger right now. We've faced a lot of issues over the past few years, and I'm sure people wish it was anyone but Facebook putting this idea forward".

This was an explicit recognition of the relationship between the political environment and reputation. In this case, Zuckerberg realised that Facebook's engagement with government has been tainted by its reputation.

In Facebook's case, what was once a stellar reputation has been dented by a series of scandals, but also complaints that it has not done enough or taken action quickly enough to deal with the problems faced. This has given the politicians "permission" to start taking action. As a result, Facebook is not being listened to, and this could do it real damage, both in terms of political intervention (taxes, regulation etc.), but also by not being allowed to progress new ideas or concepts that require some political or regulatory agreement. The example of Facebook serves as a stark warning to others.

Sometimes you need to stand up

Not all political comment is welcome, and sometimes politicians simply get things wrong. There can be a tendency to steer away from responding. The risks may be considered too high when balanced against the, often limited, upside. "Wounded" politicians can, after all, tend to respond in quite forceful and vocal manners, impacting directly on reputations. There can be a risk-adverse response which prioritises avoiding the prospect of escalating the problem beyond all recognition. That can happen if the politicians involved really feel as if they are being singled out or if the reaction is much too extreme.

Very often, all that is needed is for the politicians to hear the other side of the story. Reaching out to provide balance and perspective and to correct anything that is actually wrong is more than acceptable, and should be encouraged. Tone and content are key, but the principle of responding is correct. Poor information and misguided opinions can be shared amongst political or policy audiences, just as they can with any others. Unless something is done about them, then they risk becoming the accepted wisdom. That then becomes even more difficult to correct.

It is right to consider some of these approaches:

- Do not "hide" behind trade or membership bodies – instead, be prepared to strike a different line, if needed. Governments always want to hear from organisations directly as they too appreciate the limitations of just having a collective approach.
- Use any political information and monitoring – to ensure that the organisation knows what people are saying about them and their issues. Only when armed with this level of detail can consideration be given about whether to and how to respond.
- Convey the "criticism" in the right way – there may be an instinct to be clear and forceful, making demands for retraction etc. Senior leaders can often push for this type of response because the comments made by a politician seem to be a slur on their approach or strategy – i.e., directly of them. A more personal, lower-key approach is always better rather than simply "shouting" through the media.
- Be prepared to push for some form of redress – not in any financial way, but clarification in a future debate or even some assistance on one of your issues in the future. Do not start with a mindset that has the politicians tagged as "enemies" or "opponents". They may turn out to be your new best friends!
- Remember, status isn't everything – that means treating new elected representatives in the same manner as more established voices. A bad impression allowed to fester from the very outset can be hugely damaging, especially if those people go on to have bright careers. In other words, don't dismiss anyone just because they are not important now. Politicians can often have long careers.

Leaders should not be afraid to defend themselves and their organisations. It is often a case of getting information to people at the right time. But if they are not prepared to defend themselves, then no one else will.

> *Lesson – Do not confuse deference with an inability to stand up for yourself and your organisation*

Overall

Political audiences are more critical to reputation than many leaders give them credit for. I always advocate a pro-active approach to political and policy-making audiences. This brings better results, but also requirements in terms of consideration of their needs and priorities, not just the leaders' own. If it looks like a leader is being self-centred and only building the relationship for their own selfish ends, then the relationship is put at risk. Such a transactional exchange is not really a relationship at all, and will have no long-term future. Instead, the engagement needs to consider the pressures on politicians – timescales, who may be making demands on them, what they need to deliver etc.

There are a number of potential pitfalls that increase any organisation's level of political risk and, in turn, potential reputation damage:

- *Not listening to government* – Simply not paying attention to what government is saying and doing means organisations have little idea about what the government's policy priorities are, what its direction of travel is and what is likely to come up. The lack of information means that they are ill-prepared to make the most of opportunities or respond to potential threats. It is the surprise attack that can be most damaging.
- *Detaching the organisation from public policy* – Simply assuming that any organisation complies fully with the latest regulations is not enough to prevent problems arising. Leaving policy development up to officials and politicians can lead to unintended consequences. They need outside expertise to inform their policy development. Not engaging means that new policies can blindside an organisation.
- *Thinking any organisation is bigger than the politicians* – Answering back through the media or in the forum of a committee or during an inquiry is rarely wise. Even the most popular brands can rarely withstand the consistent attacks politicians can inflict. Entering listening and engaging modes is more useful than attack, however unjustified you believe the criticisms are.
- *Not thinking like a politician* – The need to be elected makes politicians different from the rest of us. This can influence what questions

will come your way, how an organisation will be treated and what options are open to it. Failing to think like politicians and understand their motivations and needs puts an organisation at a disadvantage. Politicians will rarely behave in the way that a business would, for instance, and if anyone thinks they will, then they will make mistakes.

- *Not having any political friends or allies* – Networks are needed in all walks of life, and political engagement is no different. Developing a political network can be as straightforward as starting with local elected representatives and then widening it over time. This network can help provide advice and guidance if things do go wrong, and may even be prepared to stand up for you in times of difficulty.

- *The classic climb-down* – Eventually, after all the gnashing of teeth and general wailing in the media, organisations end up making changes or having to comply in any case. All this extends the period of risk and uncertainty, inflicts more reputational damage and shows weakness. That is the ultimate irony in itself – in an attempt to look strong and fight back, the ultimate outcome is one of weakness. This is not to say that organisations should not stand up for themselves, but the initial assessment needs to be carefully considered, rather than knee-jerk. If leaders, in particular, are under fire, then that can be challenging to achieve.

If these pitfalls can be avoided, then a political risk profile looks much more manageable. Whilst there are no short cuts to building political trust, the investment is worth the effort.

However, unless you consider your reputation from a political perspective, you are failing to manage your risks effectively.

Notes

1 Ramzey (2018) (www.nytimes.com/2018/04/11/us/mark-zuckerberg-senate-hearing-notes.html).
2 Anderson (2018). (http://data.parliament.uk/writtenevidence/committeeevidence.svc/evidencedocument/international-development-committee/sexual-exploitation-and-abuse-in-the-aid-sector/written/81287.html).
3 ITV News (2018) (www.youtube.com/watch?v=HGGkt4ycoBs).

4 Wearden (2018) (www.theguardian.com/business/live/2018/may/02/tsb-ques-
tions-mps-it-meltdown-eurozone-economy-uk-construction-business-live?page
=with:block-5ae9bf65e4b0f016ba5854b5#block-5ae9bf65e4b0f016ba5854b5).
5 Transport Select Committee (2020) (https://committees.parliament.uk/work
/221/coronavirus-implications-for-transport/news/115136/committee-report-con-
demns-behaviour-of-british-airways/).

References

Austin Ramzey, 'Mark Zuckerberg's own data disclosed after senate hearing:
His notes', *The New York Times*, 11 April 2018.

Graeme Wearden, 'MPs slam TSB boss's complacency over IT fiasco – As it
happened', *The Guardian*, 2 May 2018.

ITV News, 'TSB boss Paul Pester under attack from MPs following IT chaos',
2 May 2018.

Transport Select Committee, *The Impact of the Coronavirus Pandemic on the
Aviation Sector*, 13 June 2020.

William Anderson, 'Written evidence submitted by Mr William Anderson',
International Development Select Committee inquiry into Sexual
exploitation and abuse in the aid sector, 31 July 2018.

6

ANTICIPATING THE ATTACK

If an attack is coming, what can you do to protect yourself, and what are the best ways of maintaining your reputation?

Some of what needs to be done can be quite mundane, but is focused on being able to "hand on heart" explain your actions. That means having the processes, systems and people in place, but alongside good record keeping. Aside from being very necessary in the event of any form of regulatory intervention, good record keeping also allows responses to be accurate when stakeholders come looking for answers.

The need to be accurate in responses may seem blatantly obvious, but the reality is that trying to pull together the details of an issue at short notice under media pressure is no easy task. It is the sort of situation where mistakes can easily creep in. If those mistakes are revealed, then the level of reputational damage increases further.

There is a clear need to have internal policies and procedures in place, but a major task is making sure they are followed. Part of this is having

DOI: 10.4324/9781003293880-7

a regularly updated crisis plan in place. The key aspects of any good plan are that it should:

- Be short and concise, making it useable under pressure.
- Include team and contact details.
- Assign roles and responsibilities, internal and external.
- Allow access to key materials.
- Explain processes to follow.
- Provide a stakeholder list, with contact details, to facilitate engagement.
- Be stored/saved in a place where it can easily be found.

Sadly, it is too easy to lose count of incidents of abuse, misogyny and racism across all types of organisations and all sectors. Sometimes this is down to the behaviour of one person, but often the culture of an organisation has allowed the incidents to take place. Behaviour like this may sometimes be accepted. On other occasions, steps may be taken to quietly remove someone, but the culture may not be challenged.

It can only be hoped that with movements such as #MeToo and Black Lives Matter, we are entering a new phase where such behaviour is simply unacceptable. But even if that is the case, it is necessary to have policies in place to clearly state what is and is not acceptable so that if poor behaviour is encountered, action can be taken swiftly. If the abuse becomes a reputational matter, then the organisation will at least be able to map out a full response covering everything from the aims of the organisation through to the policies in place which have enabled immediate and decisive action. It is the poor behaviour of an individual rather than the culture of the whole organisation which is at fault.

There are occasions when organisations try to gain credibility, and add to their reputations, by associating themselves with a movement. In the case of Black Lives Matter, it appeared that many major corporate players could not wait to state their support for the movement. Many chose, for instance, to post black squares on Instagram on Blackout Tuesday to show solidarity.

But that only has resonance and meaning if the policies and ethos of those companies bear out that support. Otherwise, it is nothing more than shallow spin which will actually reflect badly on them if examples of poor behaviour come to light.

One such example concerns L'Oréal Paris and the model Munro Bergdorf, mentioned in Chapter 4. She was sacked in 2017 by L'Oréal Paris after posting on social media about "the racial violence of white people". The company chose to post its own supportive messages for Black Lives Matter, but was called out by Bergdorf on a Twitter thread:[1]

> You dropped me from a campaign in 2017 and threw me to the wolves for speaking out about racism and white supremacy. With no duty of care, without a second thought.
>
> I had to fend for myself being torn apart by the world's press because YOU didn't want to talk about racism. You do NOT get to do this. This is NOT okay, not even in the slightest.

Bergdorf spoke to L'Oréal Paris's new president, Delphine Viguier, who apologised for the way the issue was handled in 2017, and Bergdorf agreed to join the company's UK diversity and inclusion advisory board.

The company appeared to have taken the original decision in the belief that it would protect its brand and reputation. That decision ran counter to its subsequent positions. Whilst it took immediate remedial action by reaching out to Bergdorf, it was fortunate that she was magnanimous and decided that there was more to be gained by taking the opportunity on offer. That will not always be the case.

Lesson – Keep track of previous statements and positions to ensure consistency over time

---

Any approach of this type has to consider and analyse the culture of the organisation before making supportive statements or joining a cause. This is not to suggest that only those who have a perfect track record should consider being supportive, but acknowledging where you may need to change behaviour is an essential part of the support. Rather than papering over the cracks or ignoring them, behavioural or cultural changes need to be embraced and addressed if the reputational upside is to be delivered.

> *Lesson – Take the macro view of any proposed change, then hone in on the micro to check the impact on reputation*

One of the key roles for leaders in reputation terms is to be able to consider the organisation as a whole. To do this, they should draw on the knowledge and insight of others. In *The Reputation Game*, Waller and Younger make a distinction between open and closed networks. The latter lack challenge and lead to stale thinking. The same could well be said of closed leadership teams and the adverse impact they can have on reputation management.

An organisation that allows itself to be open to challenge is one that is better prepared to manage its reputation. The concept of "truth tellers" in organisations was highlighted on the *Masters of Scale* podcast by entrepreneur, investor and author Reid Hoffman.[2] That idea can be utilised for reputation management as well. "Truth tellers" can help organisations recognise and adopt to new realities. If leaders do not listen to reputation "truth tellers", then damage is inevitable. The culture of an organisation needs to allow internal discussions to take place, but there also have to be the channels in place so that relevant information can get to the right people, at the right level. This culture needs to exist in every part of an organisation. "Truth tellers" need to feel safe and free from consequences, which requires a level of openness and transparency.

The challenge can come from within the organisation as well as from external stakeholders. Stakeholder management should not simply be about conveying key messages to the right people, but also listening to them as well. This feedback needs to be captured and conveyed so that action can, if necessary, be taken.

Too many organisations do not consider stakeholder management to be about dialogue. They should, otherwise they are failing to manage their risk. Just because the feedback comes from an external source does not mean it should not be taken seriously. The reality is that it should be taken more seriously. Critical feedback from external stakeholders demonstrates potential systemic failures:

a) Of communication – action is being taken, but the audience is unaware.
b) Of systems – action is not being taken.
c) Of listening – the feedback has been considered and ignored.

Lesson – consider stakeholder management as an ongoing dialogue

---

Thought leadership

It is critical that organisations take every opportunity to enhance their reputations. These opportunities are available to all types of organisations, and are not necessarily overly burdensome in terms of costs. Instead, they require organisations to put reputation management at the front of their operations.

Thought leadership can offer many benefits to help improve a reputation.[3] Thought leadership can set you apart from the competition and help you to set the agenda. It enables you to stand out from "the others". This means that organisations need to keep moving the agenda forward, continue to generate new ideas and respond where they can. This is how they can try to claim some space. No one is simply entitled to space.

Thought leadership is often considered as being built mainly using a written format (books, blogs etc.) shared over a range of channels (Twitter, Facebook, LinkedIn etc.). Traditional media can also be an effective channel, but it can be even more effective in person at conferences and networking events.

Thought leadership can be developed for an individual or an organisation, and the aim of being seen as a thought leader may be at the heart of a communications campaign.

The best thought leaders stick to their field of expertise and understand that they are not necessarily qualified to range far and wide over unrelated matters. Within that chosen area, they can help with horizon scanning and pushing new thinking.

Lesson – Thought leadership is not just about writing, it takes many forms

When designing a thought leadership programme, it should:

1) Consider the latest issues – being sure to respond promptly to the latest developments. This is when the potential for wider media opportunities is at its greatest, as audiences will pay more attention to immediate reactions to something new.

2) Say something new – drawing information from a range of sources and trying to find an angle or interpret the information in a way that others are missing. This is the sort of insight that policy-makers, in particular, find useful. Whether we are still living in an era of evidence-based policy making or "alternative facts", there will still be no substitute for being able to draw upon and highlight real-life experiences.

3) Bring a new perspective – space in a policy area can often be hard to come by, so the programme needs to identify and utilise individuals' or the organisation's areas of expertise. The perspective should reflect that expertise, not just narrow commercial interests. That could mean drawing thoughts up from within the organisation to inform the perspective.

4) Ensure that what is said is genuine – if a position smacks too much of political or media posturing, then it will not have the impact being sought. That sort of position can be too easily dismissed. Instead, it has to be reflective of a genuine understanding of the matter at hand and a personal commitment. Anything that can be considered opportunistic should be avoided as it will undermine your thought leadership credentials and reputation.

5) Think beyond a sector – when devising a narrative, reflect upon how the topic impacts others beyond any immediate interests or sectors. For instance, a new policy that has wider consequences will draw interest from a range of audiences.

6) Draw in others – collaborating with others can help strengthen thought leadership credentials. It may also help by "borrowing" from the reputations of others. Just be careful who is chosen, as reputations can also be damaged by association.

Just as knowing what your audience wants is a cornerstone of reputation management, so too it is for thought leadership.

Anyone aspiring to be a thought leader needs to be aware of the interests of their intended audience. Consideration needs to be given to what the intended audience wants to know. That means taking the time to find this out, which can happen informally through discussions or more formally through, for instance, surveys.

This will help to build influence. The more the intended audience is offered something of relevance and value to it, the more influence will grow. But influence also means maintaining contacts and building them over time, being proactive through networking and using opportunities to strike up new relationships.

Every effort has to be made to get thoughts to the people that matter; no one should rely on luck for them to find you. Recommendations are really useful, so ask for help from those who already have access to your main targets.

Any approach to thought leadership needs to include a strategy for growing influence over time and improving networking in areas where it may be weaker.

What should be the immediate steps to build your reputation through influence and thought leadership?

1) Take the time to identify and understand an audience.
2) Learn from peers.
3) Be the expert, the authority.
4) Develop networks.
5) Be on top of the relevant industry issues.

But even if thought leadership is adopted as an approach to build reputation, there are some potential pitfalls:

1) *It's not all about the media* – Expressing opinions through the media can bring profile and attention, but real thought leadership cannot just be about the comment. The media approach needs to build on a deeper commitment to the issues and on firm foundations. The media comment should be the icing on the cake rather than representing the entire content of the thought leadership.

2) *Have firm foundations* – Thought leadership needs to be directly related to what an organisation does. It should not be a case of simply going after the media or policy space to get some attention. Otherwise, the reaction by many will be to mistrust the comment, however well founded it is. Thought leadership should not come across as simply being opportunistic.

3) *Live the thought leadership* – Before making any sort of public announcements on an ethical or behavioural issue, it has to be clear that an organisation is abiding by the approach itself or is at least moving towards doing so. Otherwise, there are dangers of cries of "hypocrisy" or "double standards". There is little worse for a reputation. Thought leadership needs to be aligned internally and/or be already being implemented. Never get caught out by saying one thing but doing another. This is a further plea for rhetoric to match reality.

4) *Chase policy opportunities* – Once thought leadership is in place, then there is nothing wrong with chasing down policy opportunities. This means not being obsessed with media opportunities, but thinking about how the thought leadership fits into the governmental agenda. This could be through consultations, but could also be about looking for the right platforms to champion the thought leadership – policy conferences, alongside parliamentary groups, through the work of committees or inquiries etc.

5) *Develop over time* – Often, thought leadership can be considered a fixed statement, a statement of intent or an approach. Instead, think about it developing over time. It does not have to be completely definitive or "right" from the very outset. Thinking should develop over time based on real-life feedback, data and evidence. The ability to map this out over a period of time in a transparent way can reinforce the thought leadership, demonstrating commitment. A blog can be

a good way of doing this – maybe even treating it as a professional diary for a senior leader?

Podcasting

The growth in podcasts has been enormous. Initially considered somewhat a US-only phenomenon, they are now officially "booming" in the UK and elsewhere, so are being taken seriously as an effective communications channel.

According to the Audience Project *Insights* 2020 report, weekly podcast listening (as a percentage of the online population) by country is: US 34%, Sweden 31%, Denmark 25%, Norway 29%, UK 24%, Finland 21% and Germany 16%, and is undergoing continued growth.

Figures in 2019 from Ofcom, the UK's communications services regulator, showed that just over 7 million people in the UK were listening to podcasts each week. That was an increase of 24% over the previous year, and the figure had more than doubled over the previous five years.

Daniel Stainsby, Deputy Managing Director of markettiers, believes that podcasting can play a valuable role in helping organisations build a reputation because:

> communications professionals understand the power of storytelling. How it can be used to increase understanding of an organisation's values, deepen a bond with employees, tackle specific reputational challenges and differentiate it from competitors. Podcasts are a vehicle for storytelling, whether a brand representative appearing on an established one as a guest, or an organisation produces its own.

However, simply believing that podcasts are a panacea is wrong. The common mistakes identified by Daniel include:

> failing to identify the core audience and how to promote the content to them; selecting too broad a topic (it's been said the "riches are in the niches" – if you want to reach a wide audience with audio then use traditional broadcast channels); talking about your business, rather than topics of primary interest to the intended audience; and

failing to evaluate success beyond the largely quantitative metrics provided by even the best hosting platforms.

Rather, he identifies best practice that organisations should look to when considering whether podcasting offers benefits to them:

"Podcast platforms are awash with poorly conceived and under-funded content from brands who chose to dip their toe in the format, rather than approach it with the requisite bravery and commitment to succeed", Daniel contends:

> The best and worst thing about podcasting is its low barrier to entry. As a result, there are now more than one million podcast shows on Apple Podcasts alone. So, a brand should approach the opportunity presented with the same professional discipline adopted for all communications channels.

This should, he believes:

> start with an audit of the podcast landscape to determine what the opportunity is. If you conclude there's merit to publish, then establish which marketing communications channels can be used to promote once you're done so. Only then and with an understanding of what your audience wants to hear should you then enter into pre-production, with expert counsel and production support.
>
> Once produced and delivered to your audience, don't be seduced by the number of listens. Instead, be sure to conduct evaluation research to truly measure the reputational impact of the podcast content and act on the insights gleaned to inform future episodes.

When it comes to good examples of podcasting, Daniel points to the Institute of Chartered Accountants in England and Wales (ICAEW), which used podcasting:

> to position the 1.8 million Chartered Accountants and students around the world, as well as the professional membership organisation itself (which is over 125 years old), as strategic business planners that are central to building a world of strong economies.

They achieved this through "an engaging and thought-provoking brand-funded podcast called *More Than a Number*, which taps into major issues by unpacking the numbers behind them".

However, this was part of a wider brand campaign to help the profession successfully navigate various challenges facing it:

> the podcast allowed ICAEW to showcase balanced debate and prove that a chartered accountant's critical thinking and professional ethics are paramount to understanding the world today. Presented by a respected financial journalist, each episode focuses on one important number.
>
> The numbers and associated tent pole questions have wide-reaching implications and consequences, from £350 million in [the episode] "Truth, Lies and Numbers" (Will numbers always be subverted?) and $12 trillion in "Profiting from the Planet" (What's the business case for aligning company strategy with the UN's Sustainable Development Goals?) to 9.7 billion [people] in "Feeding a Growing Population" (Can we sustainably feed an extra 2 billion people by 2050?)

One of the key reasons for its success was that the podcast was successfully promoted to senior managers and key decision makers in financial roles, as well as accountants, and gave ICAEW "a channel to engage directly with its audience".

There are still many in organisations who remain unconvinced about the benefits of podcasts.

Daniel sees part of his role as being:

> to inform and educate clients about the potential presented by new communication formats, including podcasts, and where appropriate give them the confidence to adopt and capitalise upon them.
>
> One of the most effective ways of enlightening people about the potential for podcasting is to highlight how seriously others are taking it. In 2019, Ben Sutherland, Communications Director for Diageo, said: "audio as part of our strategies is hard to ignore, that's why audio and podcasts are becoming integral to the media strategies for our brands globally".

Another is to remind them how frustrated they've been in the past by journalists or broadcasters inaccurately communicating brand messages to their readers, listeners or viewers. Podcasting doesn't negate the importance of effective media relations (in fact, placing erudite brand spokespeople on existing podcasts is akin to broadcast media relations, which has been successful for decades), but it does allow you to become the publisher, without the need for media gatekeepers.

Many will champion social media and longer-form written content such as blogs for providing direct, uninterrupted channels to audiences, and the same could be said for podcasting.

Lesson – Podcasting is increasingly popular, and is no longer a fringe activity

---

Speeches

When it comes to written materials, organisations will always look at their "public presence" across websites, social media, leaflets, adverts etc. Media statements are pored across before they are issued. But when leaders stand up to give presentations or speeches, the process is not always as rigorous.

I spoke to Philip Collins, former chief speech writer to Tony Blair and now writer-in-chief at *The Draft*, about the role speeches can play in reputation management.

For Philip, speeches have two virtues for leaders:

First, a public speech makes you get your argument straight. It irons out inconsistencies and exposes errors. Second, the public occasion is one the world is watching. This is an airing for a plan, an advertisement for the company, and an opportunity to demonstrate leadership, both corporate and intellectual. At its root, business is the attempt to persuade a given set of people to buy what you have to offer. Rhetoric is the art of persuasion. It would seem strange not to take its insights seriously, yet not enough senior executives have made the connection.

The value of a well-crafted speech and investing effort in getting it right offers potential reputational benefits both to the leader and the organisation they represent. Again, as with other elements of reputation management, we also need to be aware of the competitive element. If others are taking such actions and you are not, then there is a real risk of missing out. Leaders should be taking the content of speeches seriously. Philip observed:

> The virtue of a good speech is as much in the preparation as it is in the delivery. Nobody ever had a communication problem who did not have an actual problem. It is a mistake to think that a speech is merely the articulation of a strategy devised elsewhere. The two processes should come together. The ancient authorities on rhetoric – Cicero, in particular – do not see any distinction between what we would today call "strategy" and speaking. Thinking clearly is the link between the two, and very often, I find that though I have been called upon ostensibly to write a speech, I am in fact soon rewriting a strategy.

Philip knows what makes for a good speech and believes:

> the indispensable element of a good speech is the clarity of the central message. If you cannot tell me, in a single sentence, what you are trying to say, then you do not know and you are not ready to write. The insight that is common to all the great writers in the rhetorical tradition – particularly Aristotle and Cicero – is that the "seat of the argument" makes the speech.
>
> Then, in addition to the intellectual rigour and clarity of argument, a good speech will need a display of character on the part of the speaker. Business people call this "brand"; Aristotle more poetically called it "ethos". That character then needs to show a little emotion. That does not mean trying to get the audience to weep (although some speakers manage it inadvertently) and nor does it mean offering too many autobiographical details. It just means telling a few stories, dramatising abstract material so that an audience can see the point as well as hear it.
>
> There is one more element to a great speech, which is the setting and the occasion. A great speech needs a major injustice

and a big cause. Most speeches are not candidates for greatness which is why their elevated language can sometimes sound rather ridiculous.

Some think about speeches mainly in the context of the political environment, and there are, of course, differences in approach between speeches given by different types of leaders – business, political, charity – not least in terms of content. As Philip identifies:

> the problems thrown up by business and politics are of quite different types. The fashion to attempt to take insights from one arena and apply them untranslated into another is a category error. There are also differences in the implied audience. A political speech is usually addressed to the widest possible audience because you are seeking to talk to all the people at once. Even when it is a departmental speech, you are rarely only talking to the business interest. A corporate speech is usually narrower. There will be multiple audiences, but the field is limited by the market the company is seeking. Companies have the luxury of choosing their product range – and therefore their audience – in a way that democratic politicians do not.
>
> This has an effect on the language used. Democratic politicians try, or at least they should try, to speak in an unaffected way that is comprehensible to a general public. Business language is, sadly, awful – riddled with jargon and pompous made-up phrases that do nothing more than signal that the speaker is someone to be avoided in close company.

However, there are similarities as well:

> It is important in both instances to understand the audience. Corporate speakers think they are good at this, but in truth, the compliment is an empty one. Often, I find corporate leaders do not really understand what their various audiences think because they have not taken enough trouble to find out. They should; it makes a crucial difference to what you say and what you leave out. The other similarity is that the structure of good language and good argument is the same in all cases. The principles of rhetoric apply to all

forms of writing, from a knock-knock joke through to a speech in front of the Washington memorial.

One final difference: corporate leaders, in my experience, take both too long over their speeches and not long enough. They take too long in the sense that they start too early, involve too many people and allow too many versions and drafts to circulate. Material always goes stale when it sits around for too long. Yet they also do not allot enough time for proper consideration of what they want to say. The process of writing is routinely delegated to people who lack the authority to command the principal to pay attention. Too many executives give instructions that are hard to interpret and which they have not really thought about. This makes writing impossible. Start with two weeks to go, and have a serious meeting at which proper decisions are taken. Then stick to them, and do not send the script out to 30 senior managers. No resonant voice will survive the tyranny of tracked changes.

> *Lesson – Consider the power of the spoken word as a positive contribution to reputations*

The workplace

As highlighted throughout this book, one of the fundamental building blocks of reputation management is to deliver what has been promised.

This has come across more clearly in recent years in relation to how employees are treated in the workplace. The changing nature of the workplace, especially around expectations of work for different generations, means that all employers have had to reassess the relationships with their staff.

To put it simplistically, a rewarding workplace is not just about how much you earn, but the career on offer, the ability to contribute ideas, the level of autonomy provided etc.

In the setting of reputation management, it is easy to say how much an organisation values its people, but that only works if the organisation knows and understands what those people want and delivers on it.

The Happiness Research Institute in Denmark has undertaken research into what makes for a happy workplace. In preliminary results for the Valcon Happiness Lab research,[4] the main factors explaining the happiness variance amongst those who took part were stress, social relations, job satisfaction and self-esteem.

Once this is recognised, then mechanisms can be put in place to address them. The more that organisations are thinking along these lines, the more they can attract the brightest and the best, and help retention. It is also good for their reputation.

Fundamental to many workplaces are efforts to address and improve social mobility. Some have described this as being part of the "S" in ESG. Whilst "environment" and "governance" have had plenty of attention, the "social" aspects are coming more to the fore.

Lesson – The workplace has an increasing impact on reputations

---

According to Sarah Atkinson, Chief Executive Officer of the Social Mobility Foundation:

> every business knows the importance (and difficulty) of recruiting, retaining and developing the best talent. So, if your approach is to recruit only from a narrow pool of universities and backgrounds, if progression only happens for people with the right connections and the right accent, then you are already hampering your ability to secure talent. But worse, you're probably building in groupthink and missing out on different abilities and perspectives. An understanding of what it means to be truly cost-conscious; a connection with ordinary people and communities; the determination to strive and succeed against the odds – these are skills and attributes businesses should be actively seeking.
>
> Improving social mobility is crucial for our economy and society to thrive, and employers play a massive role in this because they have the capacity and influence to make real change. We want it, we need it to be true that if you have ability and you work hard, you will be rewarded – if whole communities and geographical areas feel left behind economically, and socially forgotten, then this damages

our whole economy and undermines our cohesion as a nation. This matters for business, and so business has to be part of understanding the barriers to social mobility and working to break them down.

For Sarah, social mobility is also part of the business initiatives around diversity, equity and inclusion, which are:

increasingly recognising that to consider race or gender without also considering socio-economic background is to risk missing the point. What academics call intersectionality – having multiple characteristics that put you at a disadvantage – is increasingly being understood by businesses who take inclusion seriously.

According to Sarah, professional services firms were among the first to recognise that, as employers and a sector, the lack of social mobility was inflicting damage on their reputations:

the combination of clients looking for more than the old school tie – 85% of respondents in the 2019 Social Mobility Employers Index said they feel their clients care about the socio-economic diversity of their workforce – and a sense that business performance rests on securing and progressing diverse talent. That's not to say that professional services firms have cracked the problem yet, far from it; efforts on outreach and attraction are showing returns, but data on progression and experienced hires in law firms, for example, demonstrate that it is still very difficult to reach senior levels from a disadvantaged background.

So many organisations still have a lot to do to deal with social mobility, and until they do, reputations are still under threat. But as Sarah rightly points out – and this is true of other aspects of reputation management as well:

taking social mobility seriously may involve a reputational dip in the short term as you face up to the fact that your workforce is not socio-economically diverse and your practices may involve unconscious – or indeed fully conscious – bias. Leaders who come from privileged backgrounds have to find a way to get comfortable talking about class and money, and recognise their own privilege, while leaders who come from disadvantaged backgrounds have to have the confidence to act as role models (and understand that their personal experience is not going to be replicable in all situations).

Businesses also have to explore and adjust to the interaction between their reputation and their culture. A reputation built on excellence, on recruiting the very best, does not have to suffer if you open up your recruitment and progression to people from a disadvantaged background, but you will have to navigate some changes to your language and presentation, the cultural signals you send internally and externally about your organisation, and what your values really mean.

Recognising the problem and admitting to it can inflict short-term reputational damage, but the benefits over the medium to longer term far outstrip that. As mentioned before, there is also the prospect of "first mover advantage", which can be highly attractive.

When it comes to working out how to address social mobility in any organisation, Sarah points to the importance of gathering data and having a baseline:

> if you don't know your baseline, you don't know where to focus your efforts nor what impact they are having. Collecting socio-economic background data can seem really complex – and it's certainly true that there is a wealth of academic literature and analysis on how best to do this – but a good starting point can be to ask your workforce three questions:
>
> - When you were 14, were you at a private school, a state grammar school or a state comprehensive school?
> - When you were 14, were you receiving free school meals?
> - When you were 14, had either or both of your parents been to university?
>
> You can also ask your employees how they feel about their ability to progress in their careers, and whether they feel the need to hide their class background in work. This will help you understand the perspectives of staff from different backgrounds.

For employees to trust you enough to share this information with you, the other critical first step is leadership commitment. Making it clear that this is important to the leadership – setting a priority related to social mobility – and showing a willingness to engage with hearing the perspectives of people from a disadvantaged background and making changes as a result – these are not easy conversations, and it's not very British to talk about class and money at work, but it's essential to leverage change. Supporting staff to start a social mobility network, enter initiatives like the Social Mobility Employers Index, or working with social mobility charities like the Social Mobility Foundation to deliver outreach and work experience opportunities to disadvantaged young people, are also good ways to show your commitment and start your social mobility journey.

A recurring theme is that no single person or organisation has all the answers. A good leader knows when and where help is needed, and goes out to find it.

Overall

It may seem as if everything an organisation says and does counts in some way towards its reputation. In the widest sense, that is the case, but the reality is that the language of reputation is the language of risk, how it is prioritised and the proactive actions taken to address it. An effective approach deals with weaknesses and makes the most of strengths. It also requires organisations to identify the ways in which their reputations can lead, such as those discussed in this chapter. These contribute to the virtuous circle of reputation.

> *Lesson – Know when to seek outside help*

Notes

1 See Drewett (2020) (https://metro.co.uk/2020/06/02/munroe-bergdorf-slams-loreal-racism-post-was-dropped-speaking-12790720/).
2 Hoffman (2019) (https://mastersofscale.com/john-elkann-how-to-build-your-company-to-last/).

3 See also my blog on thought leadership for *SpeakerHub*, Thomson (2018) (https://
   speakerhub.com/skillcamp/how-build-your-reputation-through-influence-and-
   thought-leadership).
4 The Happiness Research Institute and Valcon (2019).

References

AudienceProject, 'Insights, music streaming, podcast and radio', 2020.

David Waller and Rupert Younger, *The Reputation Game: The Art of Changing How People See You*, Oneworld Publications, 2018.

Ofcom, 'Media nations 2019 report', 7 August 2019.

Reid Hoffman, 'How to build your company to last, with Fiat's John Elkann', *Masters of Scale podcast*, 12 September 2019 (https://mastersofscale .com/john-elkann-how-to-build-your-company-to-last/).

Stuart Thomson, 'How to build your reputation through influence and thought leadership', *SpeakerHub*, 18 July 2018.

The Happiness Research Institute and Valcon, 'Working paper 1: Initial results', June 2019.

Zoe Drewett, 'Trans model Munroe Bergdorf sacked from L'Oréal slates them for racism tweet', *Metro*, 2 June 2020 (https://metro.co.uk/2020 /06/02/munroe-bergdorf-slams-loreal-racism-post-was-dropped -speaking-12790720/).

CONCLUSIONS
THE ONGOING CHALLENGE

There is no doubt that it is the moment when a crisis hits that makes most leaders think about reputations. A crisis makes the costs to an organisation clear. It is impossible to write a whole book on reputation management without giving some advice on what to do in the eye of the storm when a crisis hits.

The glare of the media and political spotlights often cause widespread panic, but the approach has to be not to panic. If there is a crisis plan and training has been undertaken, then the immediate heat can be taken out of a crisis. But it needs to be recognised that normal operations will be interrupted and the senior team can do little outside of dealing with the immediate crisis, even when preparations have been made.

Mary Beth West, a leading PR practitioner in the US and co-host of the *Ms. InterPReted* podcast, neatly summarised the preparation needed:

1) Make a comprehensive list of your risks and consider what the worst-case scenario for each is.
2) Consider how big each risk is.
3) Consider who needs to know about it and when, and set out a grid detailing which stakeholders need to be informed when and in which priority order.

DOI: 10.4324/9781003293880-8

The podcast discussion also highlighted the need to think through the worst-case scenarios and research the problems that have hit competitors. A critical part of planning for a crisis is starting the internal conversations required.[1]

These internal conversations should consider that an effective response to a crisis should be inclusive and cross-organisational. You can only get the communications right if all teams across the organisation work together.

This "single voice" approach applies to external teams of advisers as well. In many cases, teams of advisers only work closely alongside those who pay their invoices – lawyers with lawyers, PR with PR, accountants with accountants etc. They get to know and understand them well, but they do not always have wider exposure across the organisation. Planning needs to provide everyone with the wider perspective needed.

This is rarely a short-term process, but that is true for reputation management as a whole. Considering the range of necessary measures we have covered – information-gathering, training, getting to know your audiences, and building teams – it is possible to see a mix of simplicity and complexity, but also the investment of time involved.

Lesson – A leader needs to consider resourcing from the outset

---

That is resourcing in all its forms, not just finance. It is certainly not always about spending large amounts of resources on communications. Just take the example of the Royal Observatory. It managed to secure a global audience for a campaign with a budget of just £550 by using Facebook Live, and combined livestreams, expert commentaries, user-generated content, search engine optimisation and media coverage.[2]

This highlights that not all aspects of reputation management are down to a sizeable budget, and instead, some creative thinking and making the most of the experts at your disposal can be just as effective.

In the case of charities, as we have seen, spending too much money can itself be a source of potential damage.

Adeela Warley OBE, CEO of CharityComms, believes that the "sector is under scrutiny as never before":

The chasm between public perceptions of how charities operate and the realities means we will see more and more of these stories about mismanagement, waste, high salaries and unethical practice.

Although trust levels are relatively high, it remains volatile and the COVID-19 crisis has revealed a lack of understanding about the role and impact of the not-for-profit sector – from government, the public and the media.

Championing the invaluable role we play and the essential services we provide society has been at the heart of the #EveryDayCounts and #NeverMore needed campaigns – which provide a powerful case for support.

Individual charities who invest in strong brand reputations – with clarity about what they are there for and who – have done well in the crisis despite the huge challenges the emergency has placed on them.

The role that ethics plays across sectors is one that should be taken seriously. "An organisation's most precious asset is its reputation, and reputation is intrinsically linked to ethical practice", stated Francis Ingham, the Public Relations and Communications Association's Director General in a blog for the Institute of Business Ethics.[3] What that ethical behaviour will look like will vary from sector to sector, but the principle is an important and critical one.

Considering the steps that charities should take in thinking about protecting their reputations, Adeela believes that:

some charities seem to have a shiny Teflon reputation which carries them into our hearts, minds and wallets, and them into the corridors of power, while others struggle to get their story heard whilst looking over their shoulders for the next reputational iceberg waiting to trend. Too often our focus is on the bad stuff – when the real work and value to your organisation is building not just a resilient brand reputation, but an engaging one capable of withstanding the bad and putting you on the front foot.

But what are the practical steps that should be taken? For Adeela, these are:

- Audience – "identifying and focusing your investment on the audiences who are critical to helping you achieve your goals, understanding how they interact with you and how you can make it an even easier and more rewarding experience".
- Clear brand messages – "promoting the products and services which speak to their preferences – how they like to fundraise with you, give their voice to support your campaigns, policy positions and services".
- Communications – "creating relevant content for your audiences, prioritising the channels where they are, making sure it's all seen to come from one organisation with a common goal; done well, it provides a powerful context to each individual activity and draws on organisational strengths".

But above all else for Adeela, the most critical element is "building trust", so:

> this is not about pumping out banal value statements or grandiose claims – it's about a clear articulation of purpose and impact – it will be the reason people believe what you say, and should underpin all your communication, Without it, it's a waste time. Good brands are the truth told well, not overpromising or papering over the cracks.

In taking the steps in advance of a potential crisis and in trying to avoid one, she suggests that charities:

1) Know your vulnerabilities – forewarned is fore-armed. Create a risk register for your charity which rates the risks, identifies who owns these risks and will lead on the mitigation plan.
2) Get organised – agree the response team roles and remits, CEO, senior management team (SMT), legal and specialists, and ensure they understand their roles and responsibilities.
3) Create a practical protocol and contact lists.
4) Identify and train good spokespeople.
5) Foster a comms culture where information is shared rapidly and people have the confidence to voice concerns.

6) Raise awareness and cascade information to all stakeholders: SMT, board, patrons, staff, volunteers, supporters, public, media, government – regular, reliable and transparent updates will make them feel valued and confident in your response and their own communications with the outside world.

7) Agree crisis alert systems – early warning and speedy sign-off.

8) Ensure you have monitoring systems in place so you can keep an eye on the conversation as it unfolds and respond in real time.

9) Review how you did, and capture lessons and update your plans for next time

10) Don't forget to share good news with your stakeholders – tell them how well you managed the crisis, what you learned and what you have put right.

As you can see from this list, whilst Adeela was focusing on charities in our discussion, the lessons can be applied across sectors.

Her useful summary would be to:

- Build a strong and engaging brand – it's the bedrock of public trust and puts you on the front foot.
- Prepare, prepare, prepare your crisis PR plan long before trouble hits; a pro-active approach is vital.
- Create a communications culture where information is shared with all your key stakeholders and people feel confident to speak up and understand their roles and responsibilities in a crisis.

One particular tightrope that charities in the UK have to walk is the accusation of being "too political". For corporates, there are examples of those who choose to make statements, but for some charities, their campaigns and related messages risk being seen as taking political sides. Adeela's view is that:

Understanding how change works, how to influence and shape social, political and economic systems to deliver positive social change is part and parcel of how charities work. The Charity Commission recognises the right of charities to campaign and that this work must be aligned with achieving charitable objects. We need to be able to show our audiences – beneficiaries, supporters and the wider world – how our campaigning provides the fastest and most efficient way to overcome the problems we are trying to solve and achieve our mission.

What makes a good leader in a crisis?

Even once all the steps have been taken and preparations made, ultimately the focus during a crisis is on the leadership of an organisation. As a general rule, the CEO should be the public face of a crisis – leading from the front, taking responsibility, explaining what has happened and what will happen.

There a number of traits that help:

- The ability to reassure a number of audiences – a good crisis leader recognises that there are a range of stakeholders to reassure and work with. The media may shout loudly and have demanding deadlines, but it is only one audience.
- Taking time to listen before making decisions – there will be no end of good advice coming a leader's way in a crisis. A good leader will listen, filter, and then decide. Instinct will doubtless play a role for many, but valuing the people around them and their advice is critical.
- Thinking about the team around them – whilst external audiences can dominate in a crisis, a good leader will think about the impact on those around them and appreciate their role in dealing with the situation. A good crisis response is not just about what is said and done by those at the top, but also what is said, for instance on social media, by teams that can be geographically spread. The culture of the organisation and the behaviours that are encouraged play a vital role. People across an organisation will often look to those at the top when deciding what is and is not acceptable behaviour. The leader has to understand the full scope of their influence.
- Understanding that they are only part of the answer – this is not just about knowing when to listen to the views of others, but also about

having an understanding that the actions of others, for instance in their sector, can have an impact on them. In a crisis, this can mean that leaders and their responses are only part of the answer.

The best leaders are those who have already thought ahead and taken the steps to avoid a crisis. For some, this means realising that their own behaviour or actions may need to change. For others, it is about listening to ideas about change that may be needed to avoid an issue.

The benefits of a crisis

Crisis can, however, bring benefits if the time can be taken to recognise them, but that requires a degree of detachment. This is easier said than done, but a period of quiet reflection in the aftermath, and some excellent note-taking, can prove useful.

> Lesson – A crisis can provide the incentive to take action

As we have seen, not all crises come as a surprise. A crisis can often be identified in advance, and preferably dealt with then. It could be related to an issue or an individual that had been widely recognised previously as a potential problem, but the ability, or inclination, to deal with it may sometimes have been lacking. The focus provided by outside interest means that action has to be taken. If it is ignored, then the damage will be ever greater next time anyone shows any interest. The crisis provides the impetus and ability to take action.

New ideas about how things are done often come up during a crisis. It is such a shock for most organisations that any "business-as-usual"-type approach ends immediately. Instead, people want to contribute, get involved and solve the issue. The crisis itself might not be the right time to do anything with the ideas, but they should not be lost or ignored.

In a similar way, outside help is often needed during a crisis, and this can help bring fresh insight and a different perspective. Under normal operations, some organisations prefer to keep everything in-house, but a crisis can call for more specialist help. If the opportunity exists to draw on this outside help more broadly, even if only for a short period of time, then it can help refresh, bring in new ideas and consider challenges in a different way.

Changes have to be made after a crisis. There is no alternative. However, solutions need to be based on insight and a determination to really make changes. Anything more superficial will simply fail, especially under the heat of further scrutiny. The promise of an "independent review" may be seen by some as a superficial attempt to deflect media attention, but they can bring real benefits. Such reviews are often conducted by outside bodies and experts in the field, not just because they are independent, but because they can bring a fresh perspective and do not carry potential in-built biases or concerns about existing relationships. This brings with it the confidence needed by senior teams to make changes.

Whilst a crisis needs to be publicly led from the top, the power of the response often relies on the wider team knowing and understanding what is happening and how they can play a positive role. There is nothing worse than a crisis only being communicated through the media. Employees need to know what to say and do, and what their role is. They are a valuable asset, and should be treated as one. If that is not recognised already, then a crisis can help break down such barriers and provide the support that might otherwise be lacking. A crisis can lead to a recognition that better communications are required.

A crisis will normally see a team pull together as they shout be your champions, advocates and generators of ideas for the future. The aftermath of a crisis provides a great opportunity to say "thank you", and not all organisations do this enough.

Ben Lloyd, Deputy Managing Director of Populus, who we heard from in Chapter 1, is quite succinct in his advice to any leader:

> Own it. Take responsibility for it, both in terms of what happened and the impact it has on your reputation. Know why it matters and what your stakeholders will be saying about it. Be open about why it happened, but be clear about what you are doing about it and why you are taking it so seriously – because you know it matters. If

it is a fundamental problem, take the lead. See how it can be turned into a reputational positive. Is there an industry-leading position you can take? Can the CEO use it as a rallying call to action? If it's operational, find out why, tell people, and tell them why it won't happen again. Don't fudge it. Don't cover it up or distract. People remember. They'll remember the bad no matter what, but if you handle it well, they'll remember the good too.

One of the critical aspects of reputation management is one of is most boring: good record-keeping. All conversations held by a board or senior team need to be properly recorded and minuted. You may need to rely on these paper trails in future when dealing with journalists, regulators or other stakeholders. It may be that you need to get stakeholders to understand your motivations for having dealt with an issue or challenge in a certain way. That paper trail can really help. The stakeholders may not agree with your actions, but at least they can see how the decision was arrived at.

And that can be critically important. Sympathy is soon lost when it appears that accidents have been allowed to happen and that the steps to identify and deal with potential problems have not been worked through. If you can talk a stakeholder through the process, then damage will be lessened, if not avoided altogether.

Lesson – Always be in a position to show your workings

What to expect of politics?

One of the themes of this book has been the importance of politics and government in reputation management. In preparing for the future and thinking ahead, this means that time and effort need to be devoted to managing political risk as well. Organisations need to plan on the basis of potential political risk and do all they can to minimise that risk. That means not just good and continued engagement over a period of time, but also thinking ahead to the future challenges and reflecting on those internally. Do you need to take action now?

What could this lead the organisation to expect of government and the way it behaves in the coming years?

- *Fair shares* – Tax is a good example where governments expect individuals, and particularly businesses, to make a fair contribution and not take "undue" action to avoid paying. The additional complication for governments is the continued rise in costs and demand for public services that need to be paid for somehow, especially in light of COVID-19. In essence, there will be more demands by government on not just businesses, but other organisations as well, to fulfil a social as well as economic role. Governments will set increasing expectations of behaviour. Add to this an apparent belief, counter to free market economic orthodoxies prevalent since the 1980s, that business should shoulder an increasing amount of the tax burden.
- *The role of regulation* – Undoubtedly, some regulations will be removed – for the UK, that is one of the consequences of Brexit – but there is a danger that they will simply be replaced by new regulations that reflect the priorities of the government of the day. Climate change is leading to more regulations. Often, as new industries and technologies emerge, governments look to address any wider disbenefits by relying on regulation.
- *Keep a constant vigil* – Unexpected things will always continue to happen. Governments always react to events, but there is a hypersensitivity around politics at the moment. That can lead to more extreme announcements and politicians trying to "out-muscle" each other.
- *Public naming and shaming* – As we have seen, politicians will use the power of the media, especially social media, to help them take action against organisations. Regulations will be imposed, but governments will also call more on the court of public opinion to try to get a more instant reaction. This might not be the stuff of mass movements, but they will try to use people power as part of the political process.

As a general approach, governments will act in a more muscular way. Electorates want to see action, and politicians need to demonstrate that or they will not be elected. Unless organisations listen to that message, then they will be unprepared for the political environment that is emerging. Organisations need to be on top of all these political trends.

Keeping it simple

There is an increasing reliance on direct channels of communications. The belief is that by doing so, messages will not be distorted, interpreted or filtered in any way. There was little doubt about President Trump's views, because of his use of social media. The Conservative Government in the UK adopted a similar approach when it expected broadcasters to carry a special Brexit day address the politicians themselves had recorded.

Trump took Twitter and made it his own personal loudhailer. Why put statements out that are bound to be interpreted or shortened by the traditional media? Why not use a channel at your disposal to get your side across, directly to the people who want to hear you?

Issuing media statements should be considered a starting point. Organisations should always have a channel to convey all the information directly as well – their website, a Medium page etc. This provides audiences with the detail and the transparency they want.

Sometimes, simplicity itself is the best option – a clear and concise approach using appropriate channels. Take this statement issued by Netflix following the sacking of an executive for use of unacceptable language in meetings. Reed Hastings, CEO, issued a long memo to all staff and was quick to take action. The heart of the statement came in the very first paragraph:

> I've made a decision to let go of Jonathan Friedland. Jonathan contributed greatly in many areas, but his descriptive use of the N-word on at least two occasions at work showed unacceptably low racial awareness and sensitivity, and is not in line with our values as a company.[4]

As Ze Frank, then Executive Vice President of Video at BuzzFeed, said: "Despite enhanced communication, there will be no significant advances in the technology of saying you are sorry".[5]

The ongoing challenge

There is no guarantee that even with the best planning in the world, a crisis will never occur. It is about planning and preparedness. But successfully dealing with a crisis is also about the investment made in reputations. An organisation that builds and maintains a reputation is better able to defend it in times of crisis.

A reputation is about everything an organisation says and does, everybody that works for it and with it, every product is makes, buys or sells, every service delivered, all finance raised and spent.

This means that the challenge of reputation management is about everything that happens all day and every day, not just in times of crisis.

All leaders need to recognise and rise to that challenge.

Notes

1 Fletcher and West (2020) (https://share.transistor.fm/s/3a8704f0).
2 *Marketing Week* reporters (2020).
3 Ingham (2020) (www.ibe.org.uk/resource/guest-blog-reputation.html).
4 Sandberg and Goldberg (2018) (www.hollywoodreporter.com/live-feed/jonathan
   -friedland-exits-netflix-1122675).
5 *WIRED* (2014).

References

Bryn Sandberg and Lesley Goldberg, 'Netflix fires PR chief after use of n-word in meeting', *The Hollywood Reporter*, 22 June 2018.

Francis Ingham, 'Guest blog: Reputation', Institute of Business Ethics, 4 June 2020.

Kelly Fletcher and Mary Beth West, *Special Edition: Crisis Planning For Business Continuity, Ms. InterPReted podcast*, 10 March 2020.

Marketing Week Reporters, 'How the Royal Observatory reached a global audience with a 'miniscule' budget', *Marketing Week*, 10 February 2020.

WIRED, 'Ze Frank on the Web at 25: 8 things to expect next', 6 February 2014 (https://www.wired.co.uk/article/ze-frank).

INDEX

Page numbers in **bold** denote tables.

Ingram Content Group UK Ltd.
Milton Keynes UK
UKHW022256210723
425596UK00011B/69

9 781032 277462